A HISTORY OF
CHRISTIAN WORSHIP

By

OSCAR HARDMAN, M.A., D.D.

Professor of Pastoral and Liturgical
Theology in the University of
London and Warden of King's
College Theological Hostel

LONDON:
UNIVERSITY OF LONDON PRESS, Ltd.
HODDER AND STOUGHTON, Ltd.

FIRST PRINTED . . . MARCH 1937

PRINTED IN GREAT BRITAIN

THE LONDON THEOLOGICAL LIBRARY

UNDER THE EDITORSHIP OF

PROFESSOR ERIC S. WATERHOUSE, M.A., D.D.

A HISTORY OF
CHRISTIAN WORSHIP

THE LONDON THEOLOGICAL LIBRARY

Under the Editorship of

PROFESSOR ERIC S. WATERHOUSE,
M.A., D.D.

THE OLD TESTAMENT : ITS MAKING AND MEANING

By the REV. H. WHEELER ROBINSON, M.A., D.D.

* * *

AN INTRODUCTION TO THE NEW TESTAMENT

By the REV. F. BERTRAM CLOGG, M.A., B.D.

* * *

THE FIRST FIVE CENTURIES OF THE CHRISTIAN CHURCH

By PROFESSOR JAMES MOFFATT, D.D., D.Litt.

* * *

A HISTORY OF CHRISTIAN WORSHIP

By PROFESSOR OSCAR HARDMAN, M.A., D.D.

* * *

THE DOCTRINE OF THE WORK OF CHRIST

By PROFESSOR SYDNEY CAVE, D.D.

* * *

PSYCHOLOGY AND PASTORAL WORK

By PROFESSOR ERIC S. WATERHOUSE,
M.A., D.D.

PREFACE

What is the nature of worship, and what is its function ? These questions may be briefly answered as follows.

God's creation returns to its Source in an ascending process of life, which attains self-consciousness with the emergence of man. In man there appears for the first time an apprehension of the goal of the movement in which his life is set ; and his sense of dependence, and of obligation and ability to conform to this upward movement and to promote it, finds expression in his diverse religious cults and in his observance of an ordered way of life. These two things together make up his worshipful activity ; so that worship may be held to consist primarily in a creaturely awareness of God, and secondarily in the expression of aspiration towards God by means of religious exercises and moral obedience. Religious exercises alone may indicate religiosity rather than worship. Moral obedience alone is morality but not worship. But when a sense of supernatural Presence, however vague in its intellectual definition, finds expression in acts of reverent approach and of dutiful obedience, then there is worship.

Man's worship of God through cult and morals
is conditioned by the standards of his knowledge of
God.   As he thinks, so he worships, and so he is.
Where his conception of God is false and imperfect,
there his morality is defective and his cult is at fault,
however great his sincerity and desire.   The true
worship of God is dependent upon the true knowledge of God.   The condition governing man's
ability to offer the purest part of that increasing
volume of worshipping life which is the product of
the activity of the immanent Spirit of God is expressed in the saying, "They that worship Him
must worship in spirit and truth."   Worship must
be offered according to the truth as it is declared in
Jesus Christ and by the power of the indwelling
Holy Spirit.   The Incarnate Son of God leads the
human family, and the lower creation from which
that family has sprung, upwards to the Father ; and
He bestows upon the Church, which is His Body, a
special power of worship and a special responsibility
for worship, which must always be centred upon
the sacrificial offering of Himself in perfect obedience once for all upon Calvary, and must always be
associated with His continuing intercession at the
right hand of the Father.   This is the differentia,
the distinguishing mark, of Christian worship.   It
is " in Christ " and it is " through eternal Spirit."
Ability to offer it is dependent upon the Christian

apprehension of God and incorporation in the Church; and every member of the Church is required to take his full part in that work which is Divine Service, according to the forms prescribed by his own particular part of the Catholic Church.

The worship of God is not only man's duty; it is the path to man's perfection. By its means alone man is assimilated to the perfect Humanity of the Incarnate Christ. By sacramental and mystical association with Him in the worshipping life of the Church he is conformed to His likeness and strengthened for obedience to His single law of love. If, however, worship is misconceived as a means to morality or resorted to chiefly as a means of edification, not only is there a diminution of its worship-value, but in becoming subjective it tends to lose something of its power of transforming life and to promote the development of the critical faculty in respect of the quality of the devotional exercises employed and the standard of their performance. Man is caught, as it were, watching himself at worship, and he suffers loss through the distraction. Purely objective worship, which is dominated by the thought and apprehension of the Divine Presence, produces, on the contrary, the reward which is not at the time being remembered and actively claimed, and yet is earnestly desired by the worshipper, not as an end in itself, but as a means to a more worthy worship.

The history of Christian worship is so long and so intricate a story that great difficulties inevitably attend the efforts of any writer who seeks to provide a brief introduction to the whole subject by presenting a summary which shall be duly proportioned, accurate, and clear. The attempt has here been made, however, in order to meet the needs of the increasing number of students who are turning their attention to liturgical study; and the author hopes that his readers will find it a sound and useful foundation for further work. He and they owe a debt of gratitude to Dr. Frere, till recently Bishop of Truro, who most generously read the book in proof and made a number of corrections and valuable suggestions.

O. H.

KING'S COLLEGE, LONDON.
January 1937

CONTENTS

CHAPTER I

CHRISTIAN WORSHIP IN THE FIRST THREE CENTURIES

I.—A SURVEY OF THE PERIOD

Christianity came to birth in a small country which was incorporated in a great and powerful empire. Imperial Rome had linked Palestine with Asia Minor, Syria, and Armenia in the north, and with the Balkans, Italy, Gaul, and Spain, and the whole of the Mediterranean coast of Africa, in the west. The Church lost no time in seizing the opportunities thus presented to it. Starting from Jerusalem, it proceeded to preach the Gospel wherever Roman ships and roads could carry its messengers. It propagated itself more quickly in the East than in the West, more readily in the cities than in the country districts, and, at first, more successfully among the poorer and less-educated classes of the people than among the cultured and well-to-do. Yielding to no danger or opposition, and availing itself of two specially favourable periods, under the Emperor Commodus and his successors from 180 to 248, and during the long relief from persecution which it enjoyed from 260 to 303, it made such remarkable progress that by the beginning of the fourth century there were probably some four million Christians in the Empire.

On a general survey of the first three hundred years of its history the Church may be said to have established its position by achieving three successive emancipations, in each of which it carried away spoils for use in its worship. First it transcended the Judaism in which it had been fostered in its earliest days ; then it successfully countered the claims of rival systems of religion and philosophy, and began to take its rightful place, clear of them all, as a religion wholly different, though in some things very like ; and lastly it delivered itself from the hostility of the Roman imperial authorities by demonstrating the futility of the policy of persecution which had been resorted to at intervals in the interest of the State. The Church carried over from Judaism a large contribution to the worship which it evolved by its own genius ; it frankly recognized in the thought and practice of some of its Greek competitors parallels to certain elements in its own use ; and finally, the Roman system of administration and the architecture of its larger houses and public halls lent suggestive guidance to the Church in the grading of its hierarchy and the subsequent defining of spheres of jurisdiction, and in the building of its places of worship.

The Edict of Milan, issued by the Emperor

Constantine in 313, fixes the term of our first period. Until that year the Church's worship was offered by communities of Christians who, while they lived joyously in a strong sense of fellowship with the risen Christ, lived dangerously also, since they were commonly regarded with suspicion and hostility, and were liable to be called upon to share deeply in the fellowship of the Cross through acts of mob violence or of authorized persecution. The bounds of the Church were being steadily enlarged, and the worship of the Church was being steadily developed; but the conditions were often difficult and dangerous until Constantine's edict of toleration for all religions brought relief to the Christians of the West, and the issue of a corresponding order by Licinius from Nicomedia a few months later gave the same enfranchisement to the Christians of the East. Immediately there followed a period of rapid growth in many matters which have to do with the Church's worship; and though the new liberty brought loss as well as gain, there can be no question that the issue of the edict marks the beginning of a new stage of development.

II.—ESTATES OF MEN AND THEIR FUNCTIONS IN WORSHIP

1. *The Laity.* In the first days of the Church's history there was but one line of demarcation

between its members. The Apostles stood over against the rest as men in authority, representative of Christ, the Head of the Body. The others were God's λάος, His chosen people. Together they made up the ἐκκλησία, the sacred community which God had called forth from the world. Understanding from the beginning that " all the members have not the same office," they yet appreciated the truth that, since the Body is one, the worship which it offers must be the concern of all ; and the most striking characteristic of the Church's worship in the first three centuries was the fellowship from which it sprang and the corporate action with which it was offered. The Apostles, and subsequently their delegates, were the accepted leaders ; but the presence and co-operation of the laity were essential. At appointed times they met as people who had a common privilege to share and a common duty to discharge.

2. *The Clergy and their Assistants*. While the Church was still confined to Jerusalem, the Apostles found it necessary to provide assistance in the serving of tables by the appointment of seven chosen men. When they set out on their travels and established communities of Christians in the cities through which they passed, they ordained senior men (πρεσβύτεροι) as overseers (ἐπίσκοποι) in every place to superintend the worship there and

the administration of affairs, with the authority of apostolic delegates. Presently these presbyter-bishops experienced the same need as the Apostles in Jerusalem, and subordinate ministers (διάκονοι) were appointed to discharge a ministry of liturgical and administrative assistance.

The disappearance of the Apostles from the scene is shrouded in darkness ; and there is but little light on the process by which in each centre authority came to be vested in a single bishop, who presided over the presbyters and used the deacons as ministers specially attached to himself. But this threefold ministry was established in very early days, and it differed from its present use only in the fact that the proper importance of the presbyters was for a time dwarfed by the bishops and their deacons. The bishops ordained approved men to the Church's ministry, and ruled in their city-dioceses as episcopal incumbents, presiding over the Eucharist (except when they gave place to an itinerant prophet), the initiation of catechumens, and other acts of worship ; the deacons attended on the bishops, guarded the Church's possessions, and took a specific part in its worship, in particular administering the conse-crated Elements (later the chalice only) at the time of Communion ; while the presbyters for the most part functioned through the bishop. It is estimated that by the end of this period there were between

eight and nine hundred of these bishops in the East
and between six and seven hundred in the West.
Christians in country districts were generally under
the care of the nearest city-bishop, and were accustomed to go into the city for worship ; but where
city influence was weak, especially in Asia Minor and
Syria, χωρεπίσκοποι or country-bishops were appointed. In the larger cities division of the people
into parishes began to be made as the Christian communities grew in size ; and this led to an increase in
the importance of the presbyters, who took charge
of the parishes under the direction of their bishop.

The forms of ordination to the offices of bishop,
priest, and deacon were very simple in early days,
the two essential elements in each case being prayer
and the laying on of hands. After ordination
there was no distinctive dress for use in
ministering ; but ministers continued to wear the
ordinary *tunica* as an undergarment (known later as
the alb in the West and as the στοιχάριον in the
East), and over it the upper *tunica* or the *dalmatica*,
and sometimes in addition the *paenula*, which was an
elliptical or circular coat with a hole for the head.
It was only by degrees that the whole body of
ministers, the κλῆρος or *ordo*, as it was called, came
to be regarded as marked off from the λαός and
subject to more exacting moral standards and to
certain ascetic requirements, such as celibacy.

From the various classes of subordinate officers which had come into existence spontaneously in earliest times, varying locally according to the Church's need, there arose in the first half of the third century something like a recognized group of minor orders, the members of which were appointed to their offices with prayer but without the laying on of hands. These included the subdeacon and the acolyte, who at first performed some of the more menial offices that had originally been a part of the deacon's work; the exorcist and the reader, who were concerned respectively with the preparation of catechumens and the public reading of the Scriptures; and the doorkeeper, who again relieved the deacon of some of his less important duties.

III.—PLACES OF WORSHIP; AND LITURGICAL BOOKS AND MUSIC

1. *Places of Worship.* At first the Christians worshipped with their Jewish brethren in temple and synagogue, and celebrated the Eucharist at home, assembling in groups in the largest room of a house belonging to one of their number. When the inevitable breach between Judaism and Christianity had taken place and the Christians were expelled from the synagogues, they were constrained to worship either in such rooms, which doubtless came to be treated as oratories or chapels, or in quarries

and sandpits and other places in the open air, particularly on sites where Christian martyrs had met their death. Presently, in the second century, they began to build churches on the same general plan as the household chapels to which they had grown accustomed ; nor were they forbidden to do this except in times of persecution, when their churches were liable to confiscation and destruction. In spite of this danger, a large number of churches seem to have been built in the latter part of our period, worship still taking place in houses or in the open air when no church was available. Mention should be made also of the practice of worshipping in caves and subterranean chambers used for burial, notably in the small chapels in the catacombs, or burial vaults, outside the walls of Rome, where on anniversaries the dead whose bodies lay close at hand were particularly remembered.

The church, or house of God, which the early Christians built in many parts of the Empire, was known by the name κυριακόν, belonging to the Lord. It was an oblong building, having a semicircular end called an apse ; and at the opposite end to the apse was the *narthex* (porch or vestibule), which was provided for the use of catechumens and penitents. The body of the church was frequently divided by pillars into a central portion called the nave, and one aisle or more on each side. The bishop, with his presbyters on either hand, sat in the middle of the rounded end of the apse, facing down the church. The altar, which had been a domestic table of wood in the days of household worship, and later a martyr's tomb, but had now become a cube of wood, or stone, or precious metal, standing on four short legs, was placed prominently midway on the chord of the apse. It was covered with a linen cloth at the time of the Eucharist, and carried nothing but a paten, or plate, for the bread, and a chalice for the wine. An *ambo*, or pulpit, was placed on one side and nearer to the congregation, for the use of the reader of the appointed passages of Scripture.

In spite of the early Christian prejudice against the use of pictures and images in connexion with worship, a prejudice shared with the Jews and born of hostility to pagan idolatry, the wall-paintings in the Roman catacombs suggest that the churches of early days were not left entirely undecorated. Indeed, in 305 the Council of Elvira, in Spain, found it necessary to forbid representations of objects of worship by paintings in churches. At the end of the third century glass mosaic began to be used instead of fresco. Of Christian sculpture there was scarcely anything until the fourth century.

2. *Liturgical Books and Music.* The only liturgical writings in use during the first three centuries of the

Church's history were the Old Testament Scriptures; various apostolic and sub-apostolic works from which the canonical Scriptures of the New Testament were gradually selected in the second century; original hymns which first won a local popularity and were then taken into wider use; and perhaps certain essential formulæ together with some doxologies and prayers. But the greater part of the ritual at this time was improvised by the leaders of worship, whose action was sufficiently determined first by an agreed plan and later by the Church Orders. These manuals of disciplinary and liturgical regulation appeared first in the second century. At the end of the fourth century they had begun to give place to liturgical books which prescribed the actual forms to be used by officiants at Christian services. The chief of the Church Orders current during this period and known to us to-day are the *Didache* (*c.* 100); the *Apostolic Tradition of Hippolytus* (*c.* 217)—a book of special importance; the *Didascalia* (*c.* 250); and the *Apostolic Church Order* (*c.* 300).

As to early Christian music, not much is known; but the unaccompanied unisonal singing of psalms, canticles, and hymns, was a characteristic feature of the worship of this period, and the music used appears to have been an adaptation of contemporary Jewish and Hellenistic musical forms.

IV.—INITIATION AND ECCLESIASTICAL DISCIPLINE

1. *Initiation.* Admission to Church membership was never regarded as a matter of mere enrolment, but was invariably effected by a sacramental act of incorporation which conferred forgiveness of sins and spiritual quickening. When men believed on the Lord Jesus and sought to join themselves to the Christian community, they were required to submit in faith to an operation of the Holy Spirit which was mediated by the Church's use of water, of the imposition of hands, and, from very early times, if not from the beginning, of oil, together with the prayers of the officiant and of the Faithful. The administration of this sacrament of initiation was continuous with Jewish practice, and was indebted to it in its principal elements and in some of its accessory details. John the Baptist required of the Jews who desired to be admitted into the Kingdom the purification which they themselves demanded of Gentile proselytes who sought admission to Judaism. His practice appears to have been continued by the Apostles during our Lord's ministry; and after Pentecost it was carried on by them with a new significance and power. Extremely simple in form in the earliest days, it was greatly elaborated during the two centuries that followed the apostolic age.

The name by which the sacrament was generally

known, especially in the East, was σφραγίς, the seal. The term *baptism* was used somewhat confusedly at first to denote either the complete sacrament or that part of it which had to do with purification by water and the Spirit. The use of the word *confirmation* to denote the remaining part of the sacrament is peculiar to the West, and the term is not found in general use there until the fifth century, when it marks the growth of the Western practice of separating the two parts by an interval of time. Alternative terms were *chrisma*, τελείωσις, or *perfectio*, and " the laying on of hands."

Though at first the great majority of candidates were adults, children and infants were certainly regarded as eligible for admission to the Church by the last quarter of the second century, and it is reasonable to suppose that this had always been the case. The conversion of heads of families frequently led to the reception of whole households ; and Christians to whom children were born would naturally follow the example of the Jews and secure their early inclusion within the covenant by presenting them for the full rite of initiation. In the case of adult candidates it was ruled that certain occupations constituted a disqualification and must be abandoned as a condition of acceptance. Thus the rite of initiation was refused to any who were associated by trade or profession with pagan worship, or with the theatre or circus, or with sorcery or soothsaying ; while military service was not acceptable but was apparently permitted.

In the first days there was so great a sense of urgency in view of the expected return of Christ that no preparation was required of candidates before their initiation, and the rite could be performed at any time. A simple expression of desire on their part and of faith in Jesus Christ was sufficient. Soon, however, sponsors were required, to testify to the probity of candidates, and a course of instruction and of spiritual and moral probation was judged to be necessary ; so that during the second century a prolonged catechumenate, often lasting for three years, came to be observed. During that time the catechumens attended parts of the Church's worship, standing outside in the narthex, where churches were in use ; and they received regular instruction, in which both clerics and laymen shared. Initiation generally took place at Easter or at Pentecost. When the season of preparation for the Easter festival had arrived, those of the catechumens who were ready and desirous to be admitted were separated from the rest, the *audientes* (hearers), as they were called ; and they entered upon an intensive course of preparation as *competentes* or *elecit*. During this time they were subjected to examination as to their way of life, these

examinations being known as *scrutinia* (scrutinies) ;
and at the time of the scrutinies they were exorcised
by means of exsufflation (breathing in the candidate's
face), imposition of the hand, and signing with the
sign of the cross. On Maundy Thursday they
bathed, in preparation for their actual reception by
the Church ; on Good Friday they fasted ; and on
Easter Even they assembled with the bishop in the
place appointed for initiation, and after prayer were
solemnly exorcised by him.

In early days the place chosen was commonly a
stream or bathing-place, importance being attached
to the use of " living " water. But tanks and fonts
were soon increasingly employed ; and, when it was
not possible to provide running water in them, the
still water they contained was consecrated for use.
Some of them were large enough to admit of baptism by immersion ; others allowed only the use of
the equally regular method of affusion. After a
time the practice arose of building baptisteries in
convenient places, these being quite distinct from
churches and used solely for baptism and the
ceremonies associated with it. As a rule these
buildings were octagonal or circular in shape.

The initiation was immediately prefaced by the
first part of the eucharistic service, which in this
connexion lasted from nightfall to cockcrow, and
consisted of psalms, lessons, and a sermon. The

rite which followed varied somewhat in the order and fullness of its details in different parts of the Church, and the dates at which some of them were introduced are not certainly known; but the general scheme to which the rite everywhere approximated may be set out as follows. At cockcrow the catechumens undressed, while the bishop prayed over the water, consecrated the " oil of thanksgiving," and exorcised the " oil of exorcism." Then followed the renunciation of evil, " I renounce thee, Satan, and all thy service and all thy works " ; exorcism, at Rome only, by means of an anointing with the oil of exorcism or, in Africa, by the imposition of the hand (in Syria the unction of confirmation was made at this stage) ; and the confession of faith, made by the catechumen standing in the water and prompted by the deacon, who entered the water with him. Next the bishop, laying his hand on each catechumen's head, asked him three separate questions concerning his belief in the Father, the Son, and the Holy Spirit, and after each answer " I believe " he dipped him or poured water upon him, pronouncing at the same time a baptismal formula. After being anointed with the oil of thanksgiving the neophyte dried and dressed himself. The rest of the rite followed in church, where also the immediate preparation had taken place, if there was a church at hand. It included the imposition of the bishop's hand, while he prayed for the bestowal of grace ; and, in the East and at Rome, an anointing with chrism (olive oil mixed with fragrant substances), the marking of the brow with the sign of the cross, and the bishop's kiss. The bishop then proceeded with the second part of the eucharistic service, and for the first time the initiate shared in the holy mysteries and received Communion. In some districts he partook of water in token of inward cleansing and of milk and honey in token of his entrance into the Promised Land, between the reception of the consecrated Elements of Bread and Wine.

2. *Ecclesiastical Discipline.* The public discipline of the early Church did not concern itself with minor offences, but dealt with grave sins. Since the Christian sacrament of initiation bestows forgiveness of all past sins and imparts spiritual power and newness of life, it was not expected that sins of a serious nature would ever appear in the life of an initiate ; so that, when they did occur, the offender was held to have cut himself off from fellowship with the Faithful. In the first days there seems to have been a hope of restoration, on condition of repentance. The Epistle to the Hebrews, however, struck the note of rigorism ; and for a time the Church took the position that evildoers must be excluded once and for all. In the course of the second century it came to be recog-

nized that such drastic action was not according to the mind of Christ, and it was provided that reconciliation might be effected once, but only once, after the commission of grievous post-baptismal sin. Exception was made in the case of apostates, murderers, and adulterers; for them there was no return. Thanks to the stand made by Callistus, Bishop of Rome from 218 to 223, the rigorist attitude against sins of the flesh had disappeared in Italy and Africa by the middle of the third century, and one reconciliation was permitted to adulterers. Apostates who denied the Faith in time of persecution, and sought afterwards to be restored, presented a yet more difficult problem, in which again, however, the rigorists fought a long-drawn but losing fight. And at the end of our period it was recognized that even murderers might be reconciled when at the point of death.

The discipline of reconciliation (*exomologesis*), after confession had been made to the bishop, included the wearing of sackcloth and ashes, penitential fasting, public bewailing of the sins committed, prostration before the presbyters, and kneeling before the Faithful. For the period appointed by the bishop the penitent took his place outside with the catechumens at public worship, and was not admitted to Communion until he had fulfilled his penance and, usually on Maundy Thursday, had been absolved by the bishop. From the second century to the sixth the system of the " degrees," which was used chiefly in Asia Minor, provided for the methodical advancement of penitents through the successive grades of weepers, hearers, kneelers, and standers, in the course of their restoration to Communion. The severity of the penances imposed upon those who lapsed in time of persecution was often mitigated at the intercession of Confessors, who were held in honour because they had shown themselves ready for martyrdom, though not required to endure it. From the time of the Decian Persecution (250) the bishops in some places delegated the ministry of absolution to penitentiary priests, as a result, no doubt, of the increasing demands then made upon them in this matter.

V.—CORPORATE WORSHIP

1. *The Eucharist.* The central and most characteristic act of Christian worship is the Eucharist. Its dominical institution has been denied : but it remains the unshaken faith of the Church that our Lord Himself instituted the Eucharist on the night in which He was betrayed, and that He expressly ordered its observance as a memorial of His sacrificial death and intended it to be a means of sacramental association with Himself as Victor over all the powers of evil. The details of its particular

attachment to the Lord's Day, of its disentanglement from an accompanying communal meal, and of the gradual establishment of a regular order of rite and ceremony for its celebration are matters of uncertainty and debate, owing to the inadequacy of the available documentary evidence ; and the temptation to assume a uniform observance of enjoined practice and of prescribed forms in the earliest days should not be yielded to. In this, as in all other matters, the first Christians were guided by the Spirit to the full and satisfying expression of their fellowship with Christ by the development and interpretation of simple forms carrying a minimum of prescription.

For three reasons the early Christians were accustomed to celebrate the Eucharist in private houses in close association with a sacred meal. First, it was a Jewish custom to prepare thus for the Sabbath (and also for the Feast of the Passover). Groups of friends were in the habit of meeting together week by week on Friday afternoons for a social meal and religious conversation ; and when sunset arrived and the Sabbath was about to begin, the leader of each group pronounced a blessing over a cup of wine, for the hallowing of the Day of Rest. This ceremony was known as the *Kiddush* (sanctification). Second, it would appear that during His ministry our Lord had accustomed all His disciples to find in the meals which He shared with them from time to time an anticipation of the fellowship and unity of the Kingdom. The stories of the miraculous feeding of the multitudes have a special significance here. And third, Christ had actually instituted the Eucharist in the course of the last of these social feasts, shared with the Apostles only, and taking the form of the sacred meal which preceded the Jewish ceremony of Kiddush in preparation for the Passover. The usual Christian practice, therefore, at the beginning seems to have been to meet in groups at home on the afternoon of appointed days, for the social and religious intercourse provided by a communal meal, and for the celebration of the Eucharist. The order of the parts does not seem to have been invariable ; it would appear that sometimes the meal followed the Eucharist. There was also a general use of such terms as *synaxis* (assembly), *agapé* (love-feast), Lord's Supper, breaking of bread, oblation, and eucharist, which took no account of the limitations which were subsequently imposed upon them. By the end of the first century, however, the first day of the week had come to be generally observed as the Lord's Day, and to be invariably marked by the celebration of the Memorial of the Passion, which had taken to itself as the commonest of its titles the name Eucharist, or Thanksgiving.

The term *agapé* had begun to be restricted to the preliminary communal meal, and the meal itself was already separated from the Eucharist proper. Like its Jewish original, it was more than an ordinary meal, for it included the distribution of bread which had been blessed by the presiding bishop, *eulogia,* as it was called, and the use of religious discourse and reading, the ceremonial bringing in of lights, and the singing of hymns. But in spite of this it was not always a seemly prelude to the solemnities of the Eucharist, and by the end of the second century a long interval of prayer and exhortation was almost everywhere interposed between them. Thus the Christians would meet on Saturday afternoon for business, share the *agapé* in the evening, spend the night in vigil, and celebrate the Eucharist at dawn on the Sunday.

With the introduction of the catechumenate a clear distinction was made between the preparatory portion of the eucharistic service and the Eucharist proper. Catechumens were admitted to the former, which was derived largely from Jewish synagogal worship, and included readings from the Scriptures, the unaccompanied singing of psalms, and preaching and prayer. After the dismissal of the catechumens there followed the Eucharist proper, which was celebrated by the bishop standing behind the altar and facing the congregation, the presbyters on either side acting as concelebrants with him, while the deacons assisted as intermediaries between the bishop and the Faithful. The order of the service was as follows:

1. The Prayer of the Faithful.
2. The Kiss of Peace.
3. The Offering of the Oblations.
4. The Eucharistic Prayer.
5. The Communion.

The opening prayer was usually a comprehensive intercession on behalf of all classes of men. The kiss of peace was given by men to men and by women to women, as an expression of Christian brotherhood, in some places before the offering of the oblations, in other places afterwards. In view of this practice men and women were placed on opposite sides of the church, or the men were placed in front and the women behind. The offering of oblations included the presentation to the bishop of leavened bread and a cup of mingled wine and water (after the example of our Lord's use on Maundy Thursday) to be blessed by him, and of other gifts of the people, such as oil, milk, fruit, and vegetables, and additional bread and wine, for subsequent distribution among the poorer brethren. During the sometimes prolonged presentation of these offerings it became customary to sing a psalm, which was known as the *offertorium* (offertory). The paten on which was placed the bread to be consecrated, and the chalice used for the wine, were at first domestic vessels : but presently they were made of ivory and of precious metal, as befitted their sacred use. The prayer of thanksgiving, the eucharistic prayer, which was spoken aloud over the elements by the bishop, was for a long time an extempore prayer, which grew by degrees into an accepted form, known in the East as the *Anaphora* (offering) and in the West as the *Canon* (rule). It opened with a thanksgiving to the Father for the whole work of creation and of man's redemption, including in this a recital of the narrative of the institution of the sacrament ; it made oblation of the bread and wine ; and it invoked the Holy Spirit.

There is much debate concerning this last element, the Epiclesis or Invocation of the Spirit, both as to the extent of its use and as to its primary reference. Whereas some consider that it always had reference to the hallowing of the oblations and that it was common to East and West, others consider that it referred originally to the sanctification of the Faithful, that its use was not general, and that its subsequent connexion with the oblation everywhere in the East and locally in the West was a departure from primitive practice. Present information is perhaps insufficient to determine the point beyond all doubt ; but it seems clear that, on the one hand, there was no thought of effecting the consecration of the elements by the recitation of a specific formula, though the inclusion of the Narrative of Institution was regarded as essential ; and that, on the other hand, importance was attached to the operation of the Holy Spirit, by analogy with the sacrament of initiation. The consecration was, however, held to be effected by the whole prayer ; and not until the people responded with their *Amen* was the consecration concluded and the elements made ready for reception.

Distribution in both kinds was then made by the deacons, at first, to the Faithful, who stood and received the sacred Gifts into their right hands, while the distributing ministers said, " The Body of Christ," " The Blood of Christ," and the people replied *Amen*. Later the deacons administered only the chalice, the president himself administering the consecrated Bread. At the conclusion of the service the deacons carried the Elements to the sick who were unable to attend the service.

2. *The Daily Office*. Before the fourth century the Church was not accustomed to offer the daily round of prayer which is known as the Daily Office. In preparation for the Eucharist on Sundays and on the anniversaries of martyrdoms the early Christians used to meet for vigils, or all-night watches, which were presently reduced to a service at the time of lamp-lighting and another at cockcrow, with a

period of rest in between ; and on Wednesdays and Fridays, which were known as station-days, they considered themselves "on guard," and practised their devotions with special care. But their daily prayers were said privately, and at various hours according to local custom, a growing uniformity of practice tending in the direction of the times that had scriptural precedent and were subsequently prescribed for the Daily Office.

The *Didache* (*c.* 100) recommends the recitation of the Lord's Prayer three times a day ; and it was no doubt a common practice to pray in the morning, at midday, and at night. The third, sixth, and ninth hours of the day (9 a.m., 12 noon, and 3 p.m.), called the Apostolic Hours, are known to have been widely observed as times of prayer by Christians who had in mind certain supporting scriptural passages (Acts ii. 15, x. 9, and iii. 1 ; Mark xv. 25 and 33). And some who looked eagerly for their Lord's return remembered the parable which told of the cry at midnight, "Behold, the bridegroom ! " (Matt. xxv. 6), and rose at that hour to pray. Putting together all the various times of prayer chosen by devout Christians in different places, as it would seem, the *Apostolic Tradition of Hippolytus* (*c.* 217) advocates the practice of prayer on rising from sleep, at the third, sixth, and ninth hours, before retiring to rest, at midnight, and at cockcrow.

3. *Preaching and Teaching.* In the apostolic age, though the ministry of the Word was permitted to any who had the necessary charismatic gift, and there were recognized Prophets and Teachers, it is clear that authority belonged to the Apostles, in this as in all other matters. In the years that followed, the same distinction is to be observed. Presbyters, deacons, and laymen might expound the Gospel, but only by permission of the bishop, whose responsibility it was to preach and teach, in person or by deputy.

At first the great majority of Christians were lacking in education and culture, and the leaders of the Church deliberately opposed the " foolishness " of the Gospel to the wisdom of the Greeks. But with the coming of men of the calibre of St. Clement of Alexandria (*d.* 220) and Origen (*d.* 254), Tertullian (*d.* 230) and St. Cyprian (*d.* 258), the classical tradition and the rules of rhetoric began to refashion the presentation of the Church's message. Throughout this period it would appear that preaching at times of worship was always closely associated with the reading of the Scriptures, and was largely expository and homiletic, the bishop preaching from his seat. Outside the congregation of the Faithful, when conversion was sought, the preaching was no doubt mainly missionary and apologetic, and began of necessity to take account of contemporary philosophy.

Teaching formed an important part of the preparation of catechumens, and was both moral and doctrinal. The latter type increased in proportion as the time of preparation went on, being summarized at the end in a *symbolum*, or creed, which the initiate was required to repeat as he stood in the water. The Apostles' Creed, in rudimentary form, can be traced back to this usage at Rome in the early years of the second century.

VI.—THE HALLOWING OF LIFE

1. *Festivals and Fasts.* From the beginning it was recognized that the Christian religion is concerned with the whole of life ; and days, weeks, and years began to be marked accordingly. Each day had its hours of prayer, varying in time and frequency in the different parts of the Church, but tending to grow into a system which was generally observed. Each week had its festival in honour of the Resurrection, and its station-days, Wednesday and Friday, when Christians stood on guard against evil, and gave themselves to fasting and prayer. The Lord's Day was at first observed side by side with the Jewish Sabbath ; then it gradually superseded it, substituting for the essential idea of rest that of spiritual rejoicing and worship, and requiring that prayer should be offered standing, as a token of joy. The idea of station-days was probably borrowed from

the Jewish observance of Monday and Thursday as fast-days ; and the choice of days was probably determined by the recollection of the treachery of Judas and the blasphemy of the Crucifixion.

The formation of the Christian year began with the transformation of the Jewish Passover and Pentecost respectively into Easter as the festival of the Resurrection and Whitsunday as the festival of the outpouring of the Holy Spirit. Maundy Thursday was from the first a day of solemn observance, and the Friday and Saturday fast in preparation for Easter was gradually extended ; while the whole period of fifty days from Easter to Whitsunday was kept as a prolonged feast. The observance of Easter had become general in the second century, and in the middle of the century a controversy arose between the Quartodecimans, who kept the feast on the fourteenth day after the March new moon, according to the practice of the Jews, and those who kept it on the Sunday following that day. In the end it was agreed throughout the Church that Easter should be observed on a Sunday. The only other festivals observed at this time were the anniversaries of martyrdoms ; and these were naturally determined by local interests.

2. *Marriage*. The marriage of Christians remained for some time a private ceremony, for which the Church provided no specific rite. But the

Church inevitably concerned itself with so important a matter as the marriage of its members, and it became the custom both that it should be represented at the time of betrothal, in order that it might be satisfied that nothing prejudicial to the spiritual well-being of its members was contemplated, and also that it should consecrate the union at the time of marriage, administering Communion to the couple and adding the blessing of the bishop.

3. *Sickness and Death.* In time of sickness Christians were carried to church, if possible ; for the church was regarded as a temple of healing. If that was not possible, they were visited by deacons, who carried to them from the altar their portion of the consecrated Elements after the offering of the Eucharist. The bishop and the presbyters also waited on the sick, praying with them, and seeking to bring them spiritual and bodily comfort by means of exorcism, the imposition of hands, and anointing with oil. Laymen were accustomed to minister by the same means, using oil which had been blessed by the bishop. At all times the Church remembered the sick in its prayers.

Faith in the Resurrection lent a distinctive character to Christian burial from the first. When a Christian died, his friends mourned his loss but rejoiced that he had departed to be with Christ. The Church prayed over him, while his body was washed and embalmed in preparation for burial ; it attended him in procession to the grave, with white robes, lights, and incense, and the chanting of psalms ; and it made periodical remembrance of him at the Eucharist on the anniversary of his death. In connexion with this remembrance it was customary to use tablets called *diptychs*, on which the names of both the living and the departed were inscribed. The use of cremation was rejected by the Church, and the bodies of the dead were always laid in a cemetery, or place of sleeping, where a subterranean chamber, or a natural cave, or a tomb cut out of a rocky hillside, or a grave dug in the ground, provided a last resting-place.

VII.——POPULAR DEVOTIONS

Apart from the early Christian prayer-meetings for the exercise of the gift of tongues, there is little to be added, under the heading of popular devotions, to the story of the official worship of the Church and the private devotions of its members. But the *agapé* may perhaps be regarded in this light, after its separation from the Eucharist ; and closely resembling it, though very different in origin, were the funeral repasts which were derived from the pagan *parentalia* ; while from the third century pilgrimages to the holy places in Palestine began to be common.

CHAPTER II

FROM THE FOURTH TO THE SEVENTH CENTURY

I.—A SURVEY OF THE PERIOD

The second stage of our story runs from the emancipation of the Church by the Edict of Milan in 313 to the union of the Austrasians and the Neustrians, the two divisions of the Frankish race, under Pipin II in 687. By effecting this union Pipin prepared the ground for the building of Charlemagne's empire, and, in thus assisting to determine the political future of Western Europe, he fixed the scene of an important liturgical reform.

This period of nearly four hundred years witnessed the building of Constantinople, which was completed in 330, and the final division of the Roman Empire into an Eastern Empire and a Western in 395. It saw the invasion and disruption of the Western Empire by successive waves of barbarian hosts, Goths, Vandals, Lombards, Alemanni, Franks, and Huns, who pressed across its northern borders and swarmed over all its territories, sacking Rome itself in 410 and again in 455, and finally deposing its last emperor, Romulus Augustulus, in 476. It witnessed the golden age of

Byzantine culture in the Eastern Empire, which not only survived while the West broke up, but secured for a time the control of Italy and North Africa, and was destined to endure through many vicissitudes and a long decay until the Turks invaded it and captured Constantinople in 1453. And it saw in Arabia the rise of a new religion fiercely hostile to Christianity, the Islam of Muhammad, which dates all subsequent history from the Prophet's *hijra* (flight) from Mecca to Medina in 622.

As to the Church, this period witnessed in the West the almost inevitable succession of the Bishop of Rome to the prestige and leadership which had long been associated with the imperial headquarters in that city, and a hint of the territorial jurisdiction of the Popes of later days in the administration of the private patrimony of St. Peter by Gregory I. (*d.* 590). It saw the beginnings of the work of converting the heathen invaders of the Empire, including the mission of St. Augustine to Kent in 597 for the re-establishment of the Faith which the Jutes, Angles, and Saxons had expelled when they dispossessed the Celtic tribes and drove them to the west. In the East it saw the Church enter into so close an alliance with the State that it placed itself in a position of subordination, and presently came to lose certain national groups, Egyptians, Syrians, and Armenians, on the ground of theological differences, but actually through resentment of imperial control. It saw, first in the East and then in the West, a remarkable growth of monasticism, which made a very important contribution to the Church's worship. And finally, in both East and West, it witnessed a large increase in the number of Christians and the introduction of a great deal of nominal churchmanship; a marked advance in the ordering of public worship and in ecclesiastical architecture and art; much formulation of doctrinal statement, particularly as to the Person of Christ and the Being of God; and a division and prolonged feud between Catholics (or Athanasians) and Arians, both of whom showed great missionary activity.

II.—ESTATES OF MEN AND THEIR FUNCTIONS IN WORSHIP

1. *The Laity.* The cessation of persecution and the new popularity of the Christian religion led to its voluntary acceptance by numbers of not very earnest converts; and the mistaken zeal of authorities secular and ecclesiastical enlarged and endangered the Church still further by the wholesale " conversion " and compulsory inclusion of pagans who still clung to many of their heathen beliefs and practices. To the great differences of standard thus produced among the lay members of the

Church must be added the hostilities between sections which fought strenuously in the matter of the various heresies which arose during this period. These things inevitably produced their effect on public worship. A wider gap appeared between the clergy and the laity; preaching came to be regarded by many as a form of entertainment; complaints were heard of non-attendance at the Eucharist and of infrequent Communion; and, as a result, there were puritan and reform movements on the part of the more zealous and better-instructed members of the laity, who deplored the ignorance and laxity of their fellows.

2. *The Clergy and their Assistants.* Under the influence of St. Jerome the Western Church of the fifth century began to hold the opinion that the episcopate is not distinct from the presbyterate as an order, in spite of its possession of larger powers and their bestowal by consecration; and this view ultimately prevailed in the West, though it is a contradiction of the Church's earliest doctrine. In the seventh century the bishop's see came to be known as a diocese instead of a parochia. The subordination of the diaconate to the presbyterate had to be strongly asserted at times, owing to the influential position of the deacons as guardians of the Church's property and to the claims made by them as a result of their power.

In the West it was already a theoretical rule by the fifth century that bishops, priests, and deacons should abstain from the use of marriage ; but in the East the bishops alone were required to live in continence.   A further mark of distinction between the laity and all the orders of the clergy appeared in the adoption of the monastic tonsure in varying forms by the latter early in the sixth century ; and, whereas time brought changes in the customary fashion of dress for the laity, the clergy continued to follow the old use both in church and outside, and the garments they wore began to acquire an official significance and a symbolical interpretation.   The *orarium* (napkin) carried by the deacon on the left shoulder having begun to be folded and to be regarded as a characteristic vestment known as the stole, a second napkin (*mappula*) carried on the left arm took its place.   The *paenula* had not yet become a distinctively clerical vestment ; but the clergy generally used a larger form of the garment than that worn by laymen, and the names *amphibalus*, *planeta*, and *casula*, began to be used of this fuller garment.

3. *The Religious Orders.*   In the latter part of the third century numbers of Christians living in Egypt, among whom St. Antony was the chief, practised solitude and strict asceticism ; and, after passing through an intermediate stage of association

in groups for the purpose of prayer, many of these ascetics adopted a corporate organization devised by Pachomius (*d.* 346). The earliest of these three stages of growth was reproduced in Syria in the fourth century; but in Asia Minor St. Basil of Cæsarea further developed the coenobitic monasticism of Pachomius. This community life, which was in all places essentially a laymen's movement, was made known to the West by St. Athanasius, and was strongly supported by St. Jerome, St. Ambrose, and St. Augustine; in Gaul it enjoyed the special advantage of the work of St. Martin of Tours, of John Cassian, and of St. Honoratus, the founder of Lerins; while in Ireland, where the tribal organization of the people was unfavourable to the adoption of the city-diocese system, monasticism became supremely important and ecclesiastical life came to centre in the monasteries. Western monasticism was eventually fashioned into its most generally accepted form by St. Benedict of Nursia (*d.* 543), who founded a community at Monte Cassino, and gave it his famous Rule in 529.

Of all the many benefits conferred upon the Church by the monastic foundations of various types that sprang up in every land to which Christianity penetrated, the greatest was the perfecting and the unbroken maintenance of the daily offering of prayer. Everywhere the monks set a standard, provided a stimulus, and discharged a special responsibility in this matter.

III.—PLACES OF WORSHIP ; AND LITURGICAL BOOKS AND MUSIC

1. *Places of Worship*. In the fourth century churches sprang up all over the Empire, most of them new, some of them transformed pagan temples, and some of them reconstructions from the materials of pagan temples which had been destroyed. In the main these buildings were of two types, with much variation of detail. Either they continued the familiar rectangular plan of earlier days, or, less commonly, they were built on a centralized plan, the circular and polygonal buildings of the latter arrangement being met with more frequently in the East than in the West. The name *basilica*, which denoted a hall of some size and dignity, displaced the term κυριακόν in the fourth century in the case of the rectangular churches ; and by the seventh century it had come to stand generally for a Christian church, whatever its plan. In England the basilica was used in its simplest form, the aisled basilica being rarely met with ; and the presbytery, where the altar stood, was usually rectangular instead of apsidal.

In many churches the altar was now veiled from the people at certain times during the celebration of the Eucharist ; and in places where a ciborium, or canopy of honour, was set above the altar on four pillars, the curtain was drawn between the two westernmost of them. Frequently also the floor on which the altar stood was raised above a *confessio*, or excavation, which contained the relics of a martyr. In the fifth century the growing cult of relics led to the introduction of additional altars into many churches in the West, though in the East the old rule of one altar to each church was maintained. It began to be a common practice in the West to screen off the easternmost part of the nave to serve as the presbytery, the bishop then taking his seat on the north side of the enclosure and the presbyters on the south.

Towers were sometimes added to churches from the sixth century, for outlook and defence, but not yet for bells, congregations being summoned at this time by the blows of a mallet upon a board (*semantron*) hung in the church porch. By the seventh century a small font placed inside the west door of the church took the place of the separate baptistery of earlier days. Objections to pictures were still heard from time to time, but they proved of little avail. Their use became very general; and the interiors of the churches, especially in the Byzantine East, became glorious with mosaic panels of exquisite beauty and with many-coloured marble columns and walls.

2. *Liturgical Books and Music.* The most important of the surviving fourth-century Church Orders, which gave general instructions for the conduct of Christian worship, are the *Apostolic Constitutions* (*c.* 375), a work which aimed at completeness and attempted to summarize all previous Orders ; the *Apostolic Canons*, which were added to the Constitutions ; and the *Testament of our Lord* (?360–380), which is largely based on the *Apostolic Tradition of Hippolytus*. To these may be added the *Canons of Hippolytus*, which probably belong to the fifth century. The appearance of actual service-books, however, had now begun to lead to the superseding of the Church Orders. Books containing selected passages from the Scriptures and other valued writings were provided for the readers ; books containing the psalter, canticles, and hymns were provided for the singers ; and books called Sacramentaries, containing miscellaneous collections of prayers, were provided for the use of the presiding bishop or priest.

The oldest of these prayer-books is the *Sacramentary of Sarapion*, Bishop of Thmuis in Egypt, compiled in about the year 350. This important book, which was discovered at Mount Athos in 1894, contains thirty prayers relating to the Eucharist, Baptism, Ordination, the Blessing of Oils, the Commendation of the Dead, and other miscellaneous matters. The *Leonine Sacramentary*, which is attributed to St. Leo, Bishop of Rome from 440 to 461, is actually a private literary compilation of the sixth century, including material which goes back beyond Leo to the fourth century.

The musical rendering of services developed greatly during this period, in spite of the serious check caused by the barbarian invasions. From Antioch in the East, where antiphonal singing (group answering group) was adopted in place of responsory singing (congregation answering a single leader) in the middle of the fourth century, there went out such a stimulus to the elaboration of the musical part of the Church's worship that devotion was held to be endangered and repressive measures were taken. At Milan, which was much influenced by the East, St. Ambrose established a choir school, introduced antiphonal singing, encouraged the singing of hymns, and made a first attempt to reduce to a system the musical forms used by the Church. His work was developed, after an interval, by St. Gregory, who gave to Rome the musical leadership which had belonged to Milan. At the end of the sixth century Gregory reorganized the choir school which had been founded by Pope Sylvester in the early years of the fourth century, and he put into order the considerable volume of unmetrical plainsong or plainchant (*cantus planus* or smooth song) which the Church had been producing as its own characteristic music. It is recorded that Benedict Biscop, Abbot of Wearmouth, borrowed John, the precentor of St. Peter's, Rome, in 680, to teach in Northumbria the music for which Rome was then famous.

During these centuries many hymns were written, particularly in the East ; the use of musical instruments, forbidden in the East, began to be encouraged in the West, the organ appearing in the fifth century ; and the beginnings of musical notation were seen in the use of *neumes*, which were signs written above the words to indicate the notes to which they were to be sung.

IV.—INITIATION AND ECCLESIASTICAL DISCIPLINE

1. *Initiation*. During the fourth century the catechumenate was swelled not only by the large numbers of pagans who sought admission to the Church, but also by some who, having secured enrolment as catechumens, deferred their initiation as long as possible, either because of their high estimation of the benefits of the sacrament and their desire not to forfeit them by subsequent wrong-doing, or because of their unwillingness to accept the more exacting rules which controlled the lives of the actual members of the Church.   For some centuries afterwards there was a steady stream of adults

entering the Church in the lands where the barbarians had settled, and the catechumenate was therefore maintained, and somewhat elaborated, though its duration was generally shortened.

Additional ceremonies mentioned in connexion with the catechumenate during this period are the Roman practice of placing salt on the tongue of each candidate, in token of the wisdom that belongs to the Christian life ; the touching of the nose and ears with oil (later with spittle) while the priest said " Ephphatha," a ceremony which was known as the *Effeta* ; and the anointing of the breast and shoulders with oil. The practice of communicating the Creed to catechumens, known as *traditio symboli*, was enlarged in the Roman rite to include the ceremony of the exposition of the four Gospels, which were laid on the four corners of the altar, and the " tradition " of the Creed and the Lord's Prayer. The exposition of the Gospels was called *apertio aurium* (the opening of the ears), a title formerly applied to the *Effeta*. These three instructions seem to have taken place in order at the three scrutinies, which were held on the third, fourth, and fifth Sundays in Lent. By the seventh century the three scrutinies were beginning to be increased to seven, and all three ceremonies were performed together at the third scrutiny. At the last scrutiny, on the morning of Easter Even, the candidates renounced Satan and made the *redditio symboli*, or public recitation of the Creed, to the Church which had communicated it to them.

As to the actual rite of initiation a marked divergence of use arose between East and West. In the East there was a continuance of the application to infants of the method used in the case of adults, the bishop's responsibility being discharged by his consecration of the chrism used for the sealing of the candidates, while the whole rite was performed by the local priest acting on his behalf. In the West, where the imposition of the bishop's hand was held to be essential, it became the rule for the priest to baptize infants and then to await the coming of the bishop for the completion of the rite by Confirmation. The interval varied according to the size of the diocese and the zeal of the bishop, but was not yet determined by any considerations of age and of intellectual fitness for the reception of the sacrament. There was added to the rite the bestowal of white robes upon the neophytes and the placing of candles or torches in their hands ; and in Ireland, Gaul, Milan, and Africa, the washing of their feet by the bishop at the conclusion of their reception into the Church.

2. *Ecclesiastical Discipline.* The administration of penitential discipline began to be completely revolutionized during this period, changing from

rigorous public penance, in the case of grievous sinners only, to a milder private penance widely accepted in the interests of the moral and devotional life.

The office of penitentiary priest, which was abolished in Constantinople by Nectarius in 390 as the result of a scandal, does not seem to have persisted for long in any place but Rome; and, while there was no actual cessation of the Church's use of penance, which remained in the strict control of the bishops for the most part, it was usually so severe in its character that it lent no encouragement to offenders to seek it as a remedy for sin, and it became increasingly associated with the action of the civil power against criminals. Two factors, however, began to make for change. The first was that in some places parish priests were authorized by their bishops to deal with penitents, while in other districts the parochial clergy claimed and exercised this ministry. This gave it a more intimate and pastoral character; and, probably as a result, the fifth and sixth centuries witnessed the gradual abandonment of the Church's refusal to allow reconciliation more than once. The second was that in the West, and later in the East, the monastic use of the periodical confession of sins began to be known and used outside the monasteries. From Ireland especially the practice spread to Britain and the Continent in the sixth century, and there it established itself so effectually that the Church of the thirteenth century was able to give authoritative approval to the changed system.

V.—CORPORATE WORSHIP

1. *The Eucharist.*   From the fourth century to the seventh there was great theological and liturgical activity in the chief centres of Christendom, and carefully formulated dogmas and rites succeeded to the freer forms of earlier days.   Maintaining contact with one another by means of conciliar meetings, journeys on business and pilgrimage, correspondence, and interchange of documents, the leaders in these centres preserved the general uniformity of ritual structure which had characterized the Church's worship during the first three centuries ; but they also developed local variations with considerable freedom, and so produced a number of distinct types of liturgy which became characteristic of particular areas.   The stages of growth, the extent of borrowing, and the origin and significance of certain transpositions, omissions, and novel details found in these liturgies, present many problems as yet unsolved.   Their resultant forms, however, reveal their general relationship and determine their group.

The general outline of all these liturgies is as

follows. The first part, the *Liturgy of the Catechumens*, includes :

(1) The solemn approach of the sacred ministers to the altar, during which litanies, psalms, and hymns are sung.

(2) The reading of three lessons (Old Testament, Epistle, and Gospel), psalms being sung between them.

(3) The delivery of a sermon.

(4) The separate dismissal of catechumens and penitents. (In the West the adoption of the formula of dismissal, " *Ite, missa est*," commonly used at the close of any public assembly, led to the use of the term *missa* (Mass) to denote the rite itself.)

The second part, the *Liturgy of the Faithful*, includes the following elements, variously arranged :

(1) The prayer of the Faithful.

(2) The kiss of peace.

(3) The oblation, or offering of bread and wine.

(4) The eucharistic prayer :

Salutation and Exhortation, with a response to each.

Preface, Sanctus (Isaiah vi. 3), and Thanksgiving for creation and redemption.

Narrative of the Institution of the Sacrament.

Anamnesis (a connecting link, " Wherefore, having in remembrance, etc.") and Oblation.

Epiclesis, or invocation of the Spirit.

Intercession for the living and the departed.

(5) The elevation of the consecrated Elements.

(6) The Lord's Prayer, with introduction and embolism (expansion of concluding petition).

(7) The ceremonial fraction of the Bread, and the commixture of a particle with the Wine in the chalice.

(8) The Communion.

(9) Thanksgiving for Communion.

(10) Dismissal of the Faithful.

The distinctive types of liturgy that emerged during this period are four in number, two in the East and two in the West.

(i) *Eastern Liturgies*

(1) *The Antiochene Type*. (*a*) The West Syrian Liturgies; (*b*) the East Syrian Liturgies; (*c*) the Byzantine Liturgies; (*d*) the Armenian Liturgy.

(2) *The Alexandrian Type*. (*a*) The Alexandrian Liturgy; (*b*) the Coptic Liturgies; (*c*) the Ethiopic Liturgies.

(ii) *Western Liturgies*

(1) *The Gallican Type*. (*a*) The Milanese or Ambrosian Liturgy; (*b*) the Spanish or Mozarabic Liturgy; (*c*) the Gallican Liturgy; (*d*) the Celtic Liturgies.

(2) *The Roman Type.* (*a*) The Roman Liturgy ; (*b*) the North African Liturgy.

The first of these groups bears the name of a city which was closely associated with Jerusalem and was of outstanding importance in the early history of the Church. Its missionaries planted the Christian religion and the customs of Antioch in Cyprus, Asia Minor, Northern Syria, Mesopotamia, and Persia ; and when, in the fourth century, Constantinople (New Rome) was built on the site of Byzantium and was given precedence over Antioch, it borrowed its rites from Antioch, through Cæsarea, and presently transmitted them to Armenia. The norm of the various liturgies found in this group is set out in a private composition derived from the *Apostolic Tradition of Hippolytus* and included in the *Apostolic Constitutions* as Book VIII. To this must be added the *Liturgy of St. James*, which is of uncertain date, but earlier than the sixth century. East Syria is represented by the *Liturgy of Adai and Mari*, to be dated about the middle of the fifth century. The Byzantine rite is contained in the *Liturgy of St. Basil*, for which St. Basil himself may be partly responsible ; the *Liturgy of St. John Chrysostom*, which is a later redaction of the same liturgy ; and a *Liturgy of the Presanctified* (in which consecration is not provided for, use being made of the reserved Elements), which is strangely attributed to St. Gregory the Great.   And there is one *Armenian Liturgy*.

The Alexandrian group of liturgies is associated with the great Egyptian city which ranked second only to Antioch in Eastern Christendom.   Its norm is found in the *Liturgy of St. Mark*, which is to be dated not later than the fifth century.   The oldest of the Coptic Liturgies is the *Liturgy of St. Cyril* (of Alexandria) ;   and the   Ethiopic, or   Abyssinian, liturgy, for which a number of alternative anaphorae are provided, is known as the *Liturgy of the Twelve Apostles*.

Turning to the West, we find that the documents available for the study of the worship of Milan and North Italy, of Spain and Gaul, and of the Celtic people in our own islands, are all later than the close of this period.   While they do not, therefore, admit of more than a precarious reconstruction of the early liturgical history of these several groups, they suggest a vigorous independence of Rome in their development   of   the   original   common   use   of Christendom, with the possible exception of the Ambrosian rite ;   and they show some striking re-semblances to the rites of the East.   Rome stands apart, developing her rite upon the basis of the *Apostolic Tradition of Hippolytus*, in great obscurity so far as the modern student is concerned, but, as the result clearly shows, with a practical genius and a disciplined power which made for dramatic intensity, theological simplification, and literary precision. While no liturgical document remains to illustrate the worship of North Africa, many illuminating references, with some formulæ of prayer, contained in contemporary literature, suggest a measure of relationship with Rome rather than the independence of the other non-Roman rites.

The chief differences between Eastern and Western liturgies are these. In the East there is a richer amplification and suggestiveness of rite and ceremony than in the West; the completeness of the dramatic movement requires a longer time for the performance of the rite; and there is a fine poetic and devotional flavour about the language used. On the other hand, in the East the variable portions of the liturgy, which change with the calendar, are few in comparison with the variable parts of the Western Mass. From the seventh century the East developed an introductory service, known as the Prothesis, for the preparation of the oblations; and the subsequent procession of the oblations from the table of Prothesis to the holy table became known as the Great Entrance, and was accorded an almost central importance. In the eucharistic prayer the East commonly makes a fuller thanksgiving for creation and redemption than the

West; and it may be said that Eastern rites portray the whole drama of the Incarnation and present the Eucharist essentially as the Holy Mysteries, while Western rites emphasize the sacrificial value of the Eucharist. In Eastern liturgies the Narrative of Institution is introduced by the Pauline τῇ νυκτὶ ᾗ παρεδίδοτο (in the *night* in which He was betrayed), whereas the West uses *Qui pridie quam pateretur* (who the *day* before He suffered). Finally, in the East the epiclesis is regarded as essential to consecration, while in the West the stress is laid upon the words used by our Lord at the first administration of the sacred Gifts.

The Antiochene and Alexandrian types of liturgy differ in the following ways. First, the salutation before the Preface is more complicated in the former than in the latter; second, the Antiochene rite makes full reference to the Incarnation and the work of redemption after the Sanctus, whereas the Alexandrian rite proceeds direct to the Narrative of Institution; third, the Antiochene rite sometimes includes a confession of unworthiness before the epiclesis; and fourth, in this rite the Great Intercession follows the epiclesis, whereas in the Alexandrian rite it occurs in the Preface.

Turning to the West we note that, while the Gallican group of liturgies agrees with the Roman rite in its theological emphasis and in its generous provision of variable forms according to the Church's Year, it yet reveals a considerable measure of affinity with Eastern rites in copiousness of expression, in such points as the place of the reading of the diptychs and the kiss of peace, and even in the inclusion of an epiclesis in the Canon. By the seventh century the Church of Rome has provided two baffling problems for later days by the dislocation of the Canon of the Mass and, as it appears to some, by the transformation of an original epiclesis. The Canon has come to consist of a number of separate prayers (two of which are divided portions of the Great Intercession), requiring to be read consecutively, yet lacking cohesion in places ; and the epiclesis—for there seems to have been one—has been so effectually changed in form that scholars are still debating uncertainly the question of its position. A special excellence of the Roman Mass is the inclusion of prayers known as Collects, which are selected according to season from a large store, all of which are constructed on the same plan and are remarkable for their pointed conciseness. They were used in four places in the course of the service, and had their proper name at each place : *Oratio prima* at the beginning of the Mass of the Catechumens ; *Oratio super oblata*, or *Secreta*, at the offering of the oblations (said silently by the priest during the offertory chant) ; *Oratio ad complendum*, or *Post-*

communio, as a thanksgiving after communion ; and *Oratio super populum*, a final benediction. The use of the fourth Collect was subsequently restricted to weekdays in Lent.

While the clergy still stood at the time of Communion, lay people were now accustomed to kneel. Throughout Christendom the Elements were still administered in both kinds. In the East the method of intinction had begun to be used. In the West the Bread was still received into the right hand ; but in Gaul the women were required to cover the hand with a linen cloth. The chant sung during Communion was usually Psalm xxxiv. Reservation of the Elements was made for the sick, for use as a token of the unity of the Church by solemn despatch from bishop to priest, and to serve as a means of establishing continuity between successive Eucharists. In the East the remains of the consecrated Bread that were not to be reserved were consumed by children, whose innocence was held to qualify them for this privilege ; and the *antidoron* or *eulogia* (bread that had been blessed but not consecrated) was then distributed to those who had not communicated.

2. *The Daily Office*. In the fourth century the private and family prayers of the Faithful, the community prayers of the ascetics, and the vigils observed by Christian congregations in preparation

for the Eucharist on Sundays and Holydays, combined to produce the beginnings of an ordered scheme of daily worship offered in monasteries and parish churches alike at regular intervals in the course of every twenty-four hours. First introduced at Antioch in the middle of the century, the practice of daily prayer was quickly adopted at Cæsarea, Milan, and Jerusalem, and gradually made its way throughout Christendom. In both East and West the full development of the Daily Office naturally owed more to the monks than to the much-occupied parish clergy ; and St. Benedict of Nursia fixed its division and sequence for the West in the Rule which he issued in 529, and declared its worth and obligation by calling it *opus Dei*, God's Work.

Some indication of the growth of the practice of daily public prayer is afforded in the following references. Writing in his *Institutes of the Coenobites* (417) of what he had seen in Egypt and Palestine in the previous century, John Cassian describes the practice of the monks in Egypt as consisting of two daily services in common, at the end of the day and before sunrise, and three times of private prayer, at the third, sixth, and ninth hours. In Palestine the monks met for prayers seven times a day. St. Basil, in his *Longer Rules* (358), suggests that monks ought to pray eight times a day—in the early morning, at the third, sixth, and ninth hours, at the end of the day, at the beginning of the night, at midnight, and before dawn. The *Testament of our Lord* (?360–380) requires the clergy to hold a daily service of prayer ; and prayers twice a day, at night and at dawn, are expected of the order of widows. The *Apostolic Constitutions* (*c.* 375) prescribe psalms and prayers for two daily services, at daybreak and in the evening. The *Pilgrimage of Etheria* (385) tells of four daily services at Jerusalem (at lamp-lighting, at cockcrow, and at the sixth and ninth hours), intended specially for the monks and virgins, but attended also by some of the laity and even by catechumens. A short time afterwards Paula, a friend of St. Jerome, records that community prayers were said at Bethlehem at sunset, at midnight, at dawn, and at the third, sixth, and ninth hours. In the fifth century the *Canons of Hippolytus* require the Faithful to assemble in church at cockcrow daily. Various Canons in the same century make it obligatory for the clergy to say Nocturns at midnight, Lauds at sunrise, and Vespers at sunset, daily in their churches. In the sixth century St. Benedict prescribes eight separate offices to be sung by his monks during the twenty-four hours of the day and night, the number being conformed to the ideal seven (Psalm cxix. 164), theoretically by the separation of the night office of Nocturns from

C.W.—5

the day offices and practically by the continuous recitation of Nocturns and Lauds. The round begins in the evening with Vespers at sunset and Compline (*completorium*) at bedtime. Nocturns and Lauds are said together at 2 a.m. or at dawn; Prime on rising again after rest; Terce, Sext, and None at 9 a.m., 12 noon, and 3 p.m. respectively. At Rome, where conservatism delayed the introduction of daily public prayers, the observance of a daily public vigil seems to have sufficed far longer than in most great centres. The practice had developed sufficiently, however, by the sixth century for St. Benedict to make use of the Roman system in the formulation of his Rule, and Rome in turn took over the full scheme which he established in the seventh century.

The basis of the services of the Daily Office is the Psalter, which is recited in order once in each week. To the chanting of the psalms is added the reading of passages from the Scriptures and patristic writings, the offering of prayer, and the singing of canticles and hymns. The greatest of these hymns are *Gloria in excelsis* and *Te Deum laudamus*. The authorship of the former, which dates from the fourth century or earlier, is unknown; but the latter is attributed with some certainty to Niceta, Bishop of Remesiana, in Dacia (*c.* 400). The *capitellum*, or antiphon in the form of versicle and response, which was sung at its close, was added to at a later date by other capitella, among them being those which belonged equally to *Gloria in excelsis*.

3. *Litanies and Processions*. The use of litanies, in which a series of biddings or petitions proclaimed by a deacon or priest is answered by the Faithful with a refrain, appears to have arisen at Antioch in the second half of the fourth century. Though the word litany is Greek (λιτανεία, supplication), the Eastern litanies, which came to be specially associated with the liturgy, are known as Ectenae (ἐκτεναί), Synaptae (συναπταί), and Irenica (εἰρηνικά). At Rome the litany-form of prayer was similarly used in association with the procession which was made when the bishop went to celebrate the Eucharist in an appointed church called the Church of the Station; and to the refrain *Kyrie eleison* (Lord, have mercy), which was borrowed from the East, Rome added the *Christe eleison* (Christ, have mercy). After a succession of disasters in Gaul in about the year 470, Mamertus, Bishop of Vienne, instituted an annual triduum of processional deprecation and petition immediately before Ascension Day; and in Rome St. Gregory is said to have introduced a yearly procession of supplication on April 25, in place of the customary pagan procession held on that day in order to beseech the god Robigus to protect the crops from

blight. Thus the term *letania* came to be applied
in the West to penitential and supplicatory processions.

Processions have various uses, as the early
Church recognized. While they are primarily a
means of moving in a solemn and dignified manner
from one place to another for the purpose of corporate prayer and worship at the station and goal,
and may therefore be described as utilitarian, they
acquire an honorific character when it is a question
of escorting a person of rank, as for example in the
case of the bishop's procession to the Church of the
Station, or when procession is made to the grave at
a funeral. Again they were naturally made use of
in connexion with pilgrimages to shrines and holy
places, and thus came to be regarded as symbolic of
the Christian pilgrimage from earth to heaven.
Once more, they have value as propaganda and as a
means of Christian witness in the face of unbelief
and heresy, and were so used by St. Chrysostom at
Constantinople in 398, when he organized Christian
processions to counter the processions of the
Arians.

4. *Preaching and Teaching*. The general character
of Christian preaching underwent a great change in
the fourth century as a result of the changed conditions under which worship was conducted. The
gathering of large assemblies of people in the

splendid basilicas that were built in many places, the inclusion of trained orators of marked intellectual ability in the ranks of the clergy, the institution of festivals and saints' days when special preaching was looked for, and a new and widespread interest in Christian doctrine, all contributed to make the sermon a more pronounced oratorical effort than hitherto and to require of the preacher ability to give his message a literary form. Extemporaneous preaching was still the rule, however; and the great preachers were followed about by reporters, who used a method of shorthand in their work. During the troubled times of the barbarian invasions there was inevitably a decline in the standard of preaching.

In the East some of the outstanding preachers were St. Athanasius (*d*. 372), the famous defender of the doctrine of the Incarnation; Macarius (*d*. 375), abbot of an Egyptian community, who has left some fifty homilies treating of the monastic life; Ephraem Syrus (*d*. 379), a master of popular eloquence; St. Basil of Cæsarea (*d*. 379), who is remembered especially by his *Hexaëmeron*, a series of discourses on the work of creation; St. Cyril of Jerusalem (*d*. 386), whose important catechetical lectures take the form of homilies; St. Gregory Nazianzen (*d*. 390) and St. Gregory of Nyssa (*d*. 395), the former gifted with imagination and ardour, the latter with the thinker's power of logical statement ; St. John Chrysostom (*d.* 407), most famous of all, whose luxurious style combined with his intense earnestness, practical common sense, and biting irony, to win him a great popularity ; and St. Cyril of Alexandria (*d.* 444), who has left a number of doctrinal addresses.

In the West the great names were those of St. Ambrose of Milan (*d.* 397), whose life and teaching exercised so strong an influence on St. Augustine ; the learned and eloquent St. Jerome (*d.* 420) ; St. Augustine of Hippo (*d.* 430), whose literary remains include some four hundred sermons and a treatise on homiletics ; and two great Bishops of Rome, St. Leo (*d.* 461) and St. Gregory (*d.* 604).

There were also great preaching missionaries, such as St. Ninian (*d.* 432) and St. Columba (*d.* 597) of Scotland ; St. Patrick (*d.* 463) of Ireland ; Ulfilas (*d.* 604), who worked among the Goths ; St. Aidan (*d.* 651) of Northumbria ; and St. Columban (*d.* 615) and St. Gall (*d.* 645) of France, Switzerland, and Italy.

VI.—THE HALLOWING OF LIFE

1. *Festivals and Fasts.* To the festival of the Resurrection there was added in the fourth century the festival of the Incarnation. Different processes of calculation had led to the appropriation of January 6 for the festival of the Birth and Baptism

of our Lord in the East and of December 25 for the festival of the Birth in the West, both dates being already connected with pagan feasts of great antiquity. It is probable that in both East and West there were places where the observance of these respective days went far back into the third century; but it was not until the fourth century that the observance of January 6 made its way to the West, and that of December 25 to the East, with the result that both days came to be observed throughout the Church, the West associating the feast of the Epiphany particularly with the visit of the Magi. Gaul seems to have originated the observance of the Advent season as a preparation for Christmas in the sixth century.

The Lenten preparation for Easter was already considerably extended, even to forty days in some parts of the Church; and Ascension Day is found in the fourth century inserted in the course of the great fifty days from Easter to Whitsunday. In the following century it was preluded in Gaul by the three Rogation Days of fasting and prayer, as mentioned above; and in Rome Pope Gelasius added a fourth season of prayer and fasting to the seasons already observed, which had their origin in the ancient Roman practice of offering sacrifice three times in the year for a blessing on agriculture. These are the days known to us as Ember Days.

Until the end of this period the Sundays that fall between the feast of the Epiphany and the beginning of Lent, and those also between Whitsunday and the beginning of Advent, were given no special character and were not even enumerated. In the West they were known as *dominicae quotidianae*, or everyday Sundays.

Saints' days grew in number, and particular importance began to be attached to festivals connected with the Blessed Virgin. In the seventh century Rome borrowed from the East the observance of the feasts of the Purification, the Annunciation, the Falling Asleep, and the Nativity, in her honour.

2. *Marriage and Childbirth*. While no form of service has come down to us to show exactly what the Church did in giving its blessing to Christians when they married, it appears from references to the rite that it was enlarged during this period by the inclusion of ceremonies which were borrowed from Jewish and pagan customs. The presentation of the man and woman by their parents and friends, the joining of their right hands, the giving and receiving of a ring, the veiling of the bride by the priest, and the crowning of the married couple with chaplets and flowers, were all in use at this time. The Church's blessing continued to be associated with the Eucharist and the bestowal of the sacred Gifts.

There are signs of a confusion of ideas in the reception of a mother after childbirth, the true idea of thanksgiving contending with the Jewish idea of purification which was to become dominant again in the Middle Ages.   Under the influence of this idea women were required to worship with the catechumens until their purification on the twentieth or fortieth day, according to the sex of the child.

3. *Sickness and Death*.   Provision for the healing of the sick continued as in the first period, the Elements being carried from the church for Communion in the sick-room, consecrated oils being used for anointing, and use being made of prayers and formulæ for exorcism.   But the growth of superstition is suggested by contemporary references to such practices as that of anointing with oil taken from church lamps.

The burial of the dead began to betray some diminution of the confidence and joy which characterized the early Christians in time of bereavement, and there are signs of the approach of the medieval gloom and fear associated with the doctrine of purgatory.

VII.—POPULAR DEVOTIONS

The great influx of pagans into the Church from the fourth century onwards led to an increased and superstitious regard for relics and to the growth of the cult of saints. The greatest of all the relics that were treasured for their miraculous properties was the true Cross which was believed to have been found in Jerusalem in 327 by Helena, the mother of Constantine; and, since the greatest of all the saints was admittedly the Blessed Virgin Mary, to her was directed not only the honour and reverence which are her due, but much of the cult which had belonged to various heathen goddesses. The patronage and protection of the saints was sought after for individuals and groups, for towns and countries; and gifts were offered to them, lights were burned in their honour, and prayer was made to them, as to departmental gods, for specific blessings which were believed to be within their power.

CHAPTER III

FROM THE SEVENTH TO THE ELEVENTH CENTURY

I.—A SURVEY OF THE PERIOD

From the seventh century to the eleventh we have a tangled period of history to unravel. It begins in 687 with the battle of Tertry, by which Pipin II prepared for the ascendancy of the Franks and for Charlemagne's brilliant renewal of the Western Empire in collaboration with the Church ; it leads on through the political disruption and decay that resulted from the pressure of the Saracens, Northmen, Avars, and Slavs, when the Church maintained its existence with extreme difficulty ; it includes a second revival of empire under Otto the Great in 962 ; and it ends in 1054 with the final breach between the Church of the West and the Church of the East.

The history of the Franks, the outstanding people in this period, began with the accession of Clovis, who ruled from 481 to 511, and became a Christian in 496. Between his death and the accession of Charlemagne in 770 the sovereign power had passed from the kings of the Merovingian house of Clovis to the officials known as Mayors of the Palace ; the two main divisions of the Franks had been firmly united; the Saracens, who had marched victoriously through Byzantine Africa and Christian Spain, had been checked in Gaul at the battle of Tours in 732; and a great work of evangelization had been carried on among the Franks by adventurous Christian missionaries, notably by St. Willibrord of Northumbria and St. Boniface of Devonshire. Charlemagne reigned for forty-four years, and proved himself a great conqueror, a great organizer and administrator, and a great friend of religion and learning. He became so powerful a ruler and so desirable an ally that in the year 800 the Pope, with a shrewd approval of Charlemagne's political ambitions, crowned and saluted him as Emperor, an act which carried with it far-reaching consequences on both sides. Of the many scholars whom he attracted to his service the most important was the Englishman Alcuin of York, who lived from 735 to 804. Under his direction a great liturgical reform was initiated, which gave the victory over competing rites to the Roman forms of service and at the same time incorporated in those forms various elements drawn from the displaced uses.

The death of Charlemagne was followed by a series of barbarian invasions which assisted the rivalries of his successors, and led to the partition of his empire and the decay of his house. The Treaty of Verdun divided the Frankish territory into three parts in 843; the process of subdivision was continued under the influence of the feudal system, which flourished because it provided a means of security in a disordered world; and by the beginning of the tenth century the Carlovingian culture had been almost extinguished and the house of Charlemagne had disappeared. Credit for the work of restoration from the injurious results of the Northmen's attacks belongs to our own King Alfred, who reigned in Wessex from 871 to 901, and in a larger measure to Henry the Fowler and his son Otto, who carried out the same policy with the same vigour in Germany. In 962 Otto was crowned by the Pope as Emperor of the Holy Roman Empire, a second renewal of the original Roman Empire, which lasted in name until 1806.

Turning to the Eastern Empire, we find that the Saracens, who had driven in its defences in the seventh century, appeared before Constantinople in 718, but were beaten off by the Emperor Leo III. Eight years later Leo issued an edict against the use of icons in worship, and thus provoked the Iconoclastic Controversy, which dragged on until 842, when the use of icons was finally allowed. There were other differences of doctrine and practice which gave rise to serious opposition between Rome and Constantinople ; and the rivalry between them was intensified by Rome's increasing claims, for which the Frankish forgeries of the ninth century known as the Isidorian Decretals had provided fresh support. In the end Pope Leo IX excommunicated Michael Caerularius, the Patriarch of Constantinople, and the open breach thus made in 1054 has yet to be closed.

II.—ESTATES OF MEN AND THEIR FUNCTIONS IN WORSHIP

1. *The Laity.* Superstition and thinly veiled paganism vitiated the faith and practice of the laity in many parts of Christendom during the Dark Ages. The Liturgy in the East and the Mass in the West still provided the chief occasion for the assembling of the people for worship, the canonical hours, or Daily Office, being attended by them as a rule only on the vigils of festivals ; but debased interpretations of priesthood and sacrifice gained ground increasingly in the West, the people's part in eucharistic worship shrank to small dimensions, and throughout the Church there was a continued declension from the early practice of frequent Communion.

In the appointment of the secular clergy to their spheres of work, as also in the approval and election of those who were to be ordained and consecrated by ecclesiastical authority, the laity took their part. Rulers frequently controlled, in large measure, the appointment of bishops, and lords of the manor selected parish priests for the cure of souls among their people, provision for maintenance being made by the tithing of the crops and by endowment with property.

2. *The Clergy and their Assistants.* The secular clergy, who served as parish priests under the rule of their bishops, were conformed more closely, during this period, to the monastic clergy. As the latter lived in communities under the rule of their superiors with the primary object of maintaining the worship of God, so, in some places, the seculars lived a communal life as members of the episcopal *familia*, and were generally regarded as under obligation to observe the canonical hours of prayer. Celibacy was increasingly expected of them.

The Gallican custom of formally handing to men who were being admitted to minor orders some token of their office (*traditio instrumentorum* or *porrectio instrumentorum*) was adopted by Rome in the eighth or ninth century and became general in the West. The subdeacon received an empty chalice ; the acolyte at first received a linen bag, which was used by him to carry to the presbyters of the city the *fermentum*, or consecrated Bread, but later he was given a candlestick, and a pitcher for the eucharistic wine ; to the exorcist was handed a book of exorcisms, to the reader a book of lessons, and to the doorkeeper the key of the church. In the eleventh century this custom of the tradition of instruments was added to the forms used for admission to the three major orders, as an edifying ceremony. To the deacon, who was already accustomed to receive a stole and a dalmatic, there was given the book of the gospels ; to the priest was presented a chalice containing wine and a paten with bread upon it ; and the open book of the gospels was laid upon the head and neck of the bishop, to whom were subsequently presented the episcopal staff and ring.

From the beginning of this period the stole, which originally belonged to the deacon, was worn over both shoulders by priests and bishops as a scarf of honour. The amice, a linen napkin intended to serve as a neckcloth, was in common use as a liturgical vestment by the eighth century, and began to be ornamented with gold decorations a little later. In the same century the *casula* or chasuble was prescribed for daily use by the clergy generally, with no suggestion of any sacerdotal significance attaching to it. Bishops wore a white linen cap of conical shape, called *frigium* or *tiara*, by the eighth century ; and in the ninth century the *pallium*, which had been a distinctive episcopal vestment, was restricted in the West to the use of Metropolitans, upon whom it was bestowed by the Pope as a mark of favour.

3. *The Religious Orders.* The standard of spirituality necessary for the proper discharge of the first duty of the monks, the performance of the *opus Dei*, was lost by reason of the political disorder of the time and the use made of monasteries as places of refuge from a world of violence, and through the sheer difficulty of maintaining the struggle against inertia and evil desire. A great revival took place under St. Benedict of Aniane in Languedoc in the early years of the ninth century, however; and when the impetus given by him had worked itself out, a yet greater reform was instituted at Cluny in Burgundy, and a connexional system was established by which Cluniac communities in diverse lands were linked up with this one centre and put under the control of its head.

III.—PLACES OF WORSHIP; AND LITURGICAL BOOKS AND MUSIC

1. *Places of Worship.* Church-building in the East was checked by Persian and Saracenic wars during the first half of our period; but from the middle of the ninth century it revived again, on the same characteristic lines as before, though the churches were generally smaller than those of the

first great period of Byzantine architecture. In the West the barbarians, when they had finished their work of destruction, began to build on the model of surviving Roman structures. The style they thus developed is known as Romanesque, a term which applies to the churches built during the second half of this period and for another hundred years, in France and Spain, in Germany and Saxon England. Monastic churches were built in great numbers on the Continent in the massive forms of this style, with heavy columns, cushion capitals, round arches, and small windows, their ordinary plan being cruciform with an apsidal presbytery and a long-aisled nave.

In this country wood was commonly used until the method of stone building was copied from Gaul, and later from the district of the Rhine. Square-ended chancels and aisleless naves were the rule. Towers were sometimes built at the west end, where the main entrance was found; and late in this period a central tower was occasionally built, transepts being added to its north and south walls. Windows were small, with semicircular or, less commonly, triangular heads; and they were often constructed in pairs, with a dividing shaft. Characteristic marks of the style of this period are " long and short work," in which squared stones are set upright alternately with others laid flat; and

" pilaster strips," which are vertical strips of stone, used as an external ornament.

During the eighth and ninth centuries the growing cult of the saints led to a desire to possess relics in every church, and, in the West, to the practice of placing the relic chest at right angles to the east side of the altar with the end just resting upon it. Several results followed from this. The altar began to be lengthened north and south for the sake of proportion; the altar canopy, or ciborium, gave place to a canopy of honour set over the chest, but left its four supporting pillars still standing with their curtains; the whole was moved back to the east wall of the church; and the celebrant perforce adopted the eastward position, which seems to have been in use long before this date in many places outside Rome. A cross and a single light were sometimes placed upon the altar at this time, to take the place of the cross and lights which were formerly suspended from the ciborium.

In the East the greatly increased use of pictures and images in churches, and the veneration paid to them, led to the issue of an imperial edict for the destruction of these icons in 726. There followed the long and bitter Iconoclastic Controversy, which ended in the middle of the ninth century by leaving Christians free to use icons on the basis of a distinction between a permissible veneration (τιμητικὴ προσκύνησις) and a forbidden worship (λατρεία) due to God alone. Two results were seen in respect of artistic method in the East. One was a temporary realism of representation, which subsequently gave way to the use of conventional and stereotyped forms. The other was the abandonment of the use of statues and the substitution of sculpture in low relief and of pictures.

2. *Liturgical Books and Music.* As in the former period so in this, the service-books which were provided to meet the Church's need in offering its developing round of worship were designed for the use of individual ministers taking part in the services, and contained only those parts of the services which each required. There was a tendency in some places to collect in one book many or all of the chief parts of the Mass, but the complete missal was not yet found.

For the Mass there was the *Sacramentarium*, which gave the priest all the prayers to be read at the altar; the *Epistolarium*, which provided one reader with selected passages from the Old Testament, the Epistles, Acts, and the Apocalypse; the *Evangeliarium*, which provided another reader with selections from the Gospels; and the *Comes* or *Liber Comitis*, which was a lectionary including both Epistles and Gospels. For the cantors and choirs there was the *Antiphonarium*, which contained musical portions of the Daily Office as well as of the Mass, but was presently divided, those parts that were required for the Mass being collected in the *Liber gradualis* or *Graduale*, which was known as the *Cantatorium* at Rome.

For the Daily Office there was the *Psalterium*, containing not only the psalms but also some canticles ; the *Bibliotheca* (complete Bible), the *Lectionarius* (a book of selections from the Bible), the *Legendarius* (acts of the saints) and the *Passionarius* (sufferings of the martyrs), from which lessons were read ; the *Sermologus* and the *Homiliarium*, which provided exposition, instruction, and exhortation ; and the *Collectarium*, which contained the Chapters and Collects. The *Antiphonarium* (including the *Vesperale* for Vespers and the *Responsoriale* for Mattins and Lauds) and the *Hymnarium* or *Hymnale* together provided antiphons for the psalms, responds and verses to follow the lessons, and a collection of hymns.

The *Sacramentarium*, which was mainly required for the Mass, still included the forms used by bishops for the benediction and consecration of persons and things, forms which were put at a later date into a separate book called the *Pontificale*, and also the forms used by parish priests for baptism, marriage, the visitation of the sick, burial, etc., which were subsequently put into a separate book called the *Manuale*, the *Rituale*, or the *Sacramentale*.

The *Kalendarium* prescribed the yearly succession of festivals, which involved in varying degrees the modification of the services used on ferial, or ordinary, days. The *Martyrologium* gave the names of martyrs and other saints whose " birth "-days were to be observed, with the dates of their commemorations. The *Ordinale* and *Consuetudinarium* gave instruction for the guidance of the clergy in their conduct of public worship, assisting them to determine the relative precedence of coincident feasts and describing the way in which the necessary ceremonies were to be performed by both ministers and people in the course of the various services ; and the *Compotus* lent further help in computing the date of Easter and the other movable feasts.

Whereas these numerous service-books presented, at first, the distinctive characteristics of the worship of the lands in which they were produced, a process of interchange and fusion gradually reduced them to something approaching uniformity. The surviving manuscripts of this period reveal many of the original differences between the worship of Celtic Britain and Ireland, of Gaul, of Spain, of Milan, and of Rome ; and they enable us to watch the process of blending, in which Rome both gave and received. The most striking part of this process is seen in Gaul. Under pressure from Pipin and Charlemagne the Church of Gaul adopted the Roman liturgy in place of its own ; but it proceeded to embody, in the books it thus borrowed, material derived from the books it was accustomed to use, and this compound of Roman and Gallican forms presently displaced the original Roman forms in Rome itself.

The most important of the seventh-century documents remaining to us are the *Gelasian Sacramentary*, attributed to Gelasius, Bishop of Rome from 492 to 496, but representing a seventh-century compilation of Roman and Gallican elements ; the *Masses of Mone*, a manuscript published by Mone in 1850, containing seven Gallican Masses, probably written in Burgundy ; the *Bobbio Missal*, oldest of all missals, discovered in the abbey of Bobbio in Italy, a book containing an unusual mingling of Gallican and Roman elements, rightly called a missal rather than a sacramentary because it includes epistles and gospels ; the *Stowe Missal*, an Irish manuscript dating in part from the seventh century, and in part from the eighth century or later, containing in addition to the Mass an Order for Baptism, prayers for the healing of the sick, St. John's Gospel, and other matter ; the *Book of Dimma*, another Irish book, containing a Mass for the sick ; the *Lectionary of Luxeuil* (Gaul), a purely Gallican book, containing

188 lessons ; and the *Antiphonary of Bangor* (Ireland), purely Celtic, containing collects, canticles, hymns, antiphons, and miscellaneous eucharistic matter.

From the eighth century come the *Missale Gothicum*, the *Missale Gallicanum Vetus*, and the *Missale Francorum*, three sacramentaries, to give them their proper name, which contain mixed Roman and Gallican elements ; and the *Gregorian Sacramentary*, more purely Roman than the Gelasian Sacramentary, sent by Pope Hadrian to Charlemagne at his request, and enlarged by Alcuin with Gallican and other matter to form a group of mixed Sacramentaries.

From the ninth century come the *Ordo Romanus I*, the first of a series describing the great ceremonies of the papal Mass ; and the *Book of Cerne*, the interesting personal prayer-book of Ædelwald, Bishop of Lichfield. From the tenth century or earlier comes the *Roll of Ravenna*, containing forty prayers for use in preparing for the Christmas festival.

From the eleventh century come many mixed books, including for English use the *Leofric Missal* and the *Missal of Robert of Jumièges*, Archbishop of Canterbury, two important sacramentaries which show a blending of Roman and Gallican features ; and perhaps the *Book of Deer*, a Scottish book of prayers, which may well be earlier, however.

The beginnings of liturgiology appear in this

period in two letters describing the Gallican Mass
and some other rites, formerly attributed to St.
Germanus of Paris (middle of the sixth century),
but now thought to be the work of an anonymous
author towards the end of the seventh century; in
the work of Alcuin and two of his pupils, Amalarius
and Rabanus Maurus, both of whom lived to the
middle of the ninth century; in the treatises written
against Amalarius by Agobard and Florus of Lyon;
and in the work of Walafrid Strabo.

In the East there was much writing of hymns of
various sorts and making of Euchologies (books of
prayers), but nothing comparable to the production
of service-books in the West. The chief manuscript remaining to us of the Liturgy of this period
is the *Codex Barberinus* of the eighth century; there
is a series of Greek commentators on the Liturgy;
and there are also the important formulations of
the Eastern Daily Offices hailing from Jerusalem
and Constantinople.

In the eighth century the Gregorian music of
Rome spread gradually throughout the West, displacing other methods; and many schools of music
were established in connexion with the monasteries.
The music of the East showed an immense development of liturgical hymns for the Offices and a
gradual but obscure formulation of the music,
ascribed to St. John of Damascus in the eighth

century. It continued to be sung unaccompanied. The West, on the contrary, made use of psaltery and harp, crwth or fiddle, and trumpets; and the organ became increasingly popular everywhere except at Rome, where it was forbidden. In the ninth century the beginning of staff notation was seen in the use of a single red line, representing F, drawn horizontally across the page to assist in the reading of the neumes. Soon a yellow line representing C was added above this; then the lines were marked F and C and drawn black; and the addition of two more black lines produced the four-lined staff which was general until the sixteenth century. The first approach to harmony appeared in the introduction of the *organum* in the ninth century, by which the melody was doubled at an interval of a fifth or a fourth. This was rapidly developed towards the musical style called polyphony.

IV.—INITIATION AND ECCLESIASTICAL DISCIPLINE

1. *Initiation*. The rite of initiation continued unchanged during this period; but the gradual transition from the first phase of the Church's growth, in which adult initiation was the rule and infant initiation the equally regular extension of that rule, to the later and settled condition, in which the reception of infants was the rule and the initiation of adults the exception, resulted in the transforma-

tion of the catechumenate.   Henceforth it took the form of the instruction of Christian children ; while provision began to be made for the moral instruction of Christian adults in connexion with the changed method in the administration of ecclesiastical discipline.

2. *Ecclesiastical Discipline*.   The voluntary use of private confession as a means of grace (though not yet termed a sacrament) in the ordering of the moral and spiritual life increased during this period, first in the north of Europe and then in the middle and south.   Precatory absolution was the rule until the thirteenth century, though it appears sometimes to have been combined with the use of an indicative form.   For the guidance of priests in the exercise of this ministry books known as Penitentials were prepared, classifying sins and attaching suitable penances to them, with a view to punishment rather than to curative treatment, as it seems ; but, although these books suggest a rule-of-thumb treatment which had sins rather than sinners in view, there are some indications of a deeper understanding of the problems involved, and of an attempt to get to the root of the matter.   There was a growing use of the distinction, made long before by Cassian, between sins that betray fundamental disorder in the life and sins that represent temporary and less dangerous disturbances.   The best known of these

books are the *Liber de Poenitentia* of St. Columban (*d.* 615), the *Penitentiale* of Theodore, Archbishop of Canterbury (*d.* 690), and the *Liber Poenitentium* of Rabanus Maurus (*d.* 841).

From the eighth century the penance awarded by the confessor followed the reconciliation which was effected by his prayer for forgiveness, instead of preceding it as a condition of restoration to communion. The practice of allowing penitents in ill-health to discharge their penance by proxy or to commute it for a payment of money was gradually extended to others as a convenience and was presently encouraged. This was the beginning of the evil system of indulgences.

V.—CORPORATE WORSHIP

1. *The Eucharist.* This period witnessed a steady growth towards uniformity of rite in the celebration of the Eucharist in the East and also in the West. Comparison is simplified, therefore, and it is possible to gain a clear view of the whole field by setting down the predominant Eastern rite by the side of the predominant Western rite. In the East it was the Byzantine Liturgy that gained the pre-eminence. In the West it was the composite rite resulting from the fusion of the Roman and Gallican Masses which was carried out under the direction of Charlemagne. With small variations this form prevailed every-

where except in Milan, where the Ambrosian rite has been preserved to this day, and in Spain, where the Mozarabic rite persisted until the twelfth century, and was saved from extinction by being permitted to Toledo in the sixteenth century.

The following table will serve to show the differences between these resultant rites in West and East.

WEST	EAST
	PROTHESIS
	Preparatory devotions and vesting of the ministers.
	Washing of the hands.
	Preparation of the oblations, including the piercing and cutting of the *prosphora* (bread).
	Censing of the church.
	The priest, standing before the holy table, says a benediction.
	ENARXIS
	Three parts, each consisting of a litany, antiphon, and prayer.
MISSA CATECHUMENORUM	LITURGY OF THE CATECHUMENS
Introit. A variable psalm, during which the priest and his assistants join in preparatory devotions before the altar, viz. Psalm xliii. ; mutual confession ; and prayers. (These de-	Little Entrance. Procession to the holy table with the Gospel-book. Hymns are sung, concluding with the hymn called *Trisagion* : " Holy God, Holy Mighty,

WEST	EAST
votions were not accounted a part of the Mass until the sixteenth century.)	Holy Immortal, have mercy upon us."
	The priest says secretly the prayer of the *Trisagion*.
Kyrie. A litany borrowed from the East and reduced to its responses, each three times.	

Kyrie eleison.
    Christe eleison.
    Kyrie eleison.	

Gloria. An Eastern hymn (*Gloria in excelsis Deo*), which was borrowed at first for episcopal use at the midnight Mass and then gradually extended to general use on Sundays and Holydays.	
Collect. Preceded by Salutation and Response, and Bidding to Prayer, and sometimes followed by other prayers called *Memoriae*.	
Epistle.	Epistle. Known as the Apostle. Preceded by the *Prokeimenon* (refrain and verse).
Gradual and Alleluia. Two chants sung consecutively. An older type of chant, known as the Tract, was preserved for penitential use.	Alleluia.
Gospel.	Gospel.
Creed. The Nicene Creed; inserted in the eleventh century at Rome, but earlier elsewhere.	Litany, Prayer of fervent Supplication, and Dismissal of the Catechumens.

WEST	EAST
MISSA FIDELIUM	LITURGY OF THE FAITHFUL
I	I
Salutation, Response, and Bidding to Prayer. The Prayer of the Faithful that formerly followed has disappeared.	Prayers of the Faithful. The deacon recites a short litany twice, while the priest says two prayers secretly.
Offertory. The offering of the oblations, while the offertory chant is sung. The blessing of incense and the censing of the oblations; the washing of the priest's hands. A prayer of oblation; and the *Oratio super oblata*, or *Secreta*.	Great Entrance and Offertory. A prayer is said secretly; the holy table, the sanctuary, the icons, the people, and the oblations, are censed; the oblations are carried from the table of Prothesis to the holy table; the choir meanwhile sings the Cherubic Hymn. Then follows the secret Prayer of the *Proskomide* (offering), accompanied by a litany.
	Kiss of Peace.
	Creed (Nicene).
II	II
INTRODUCTION TO CANON	ANAPHORA
Salutation, Response, Exhortation.	Salutation, Response, Exhortation,
Preface (variable).	Preface (invariable, and said secretly, except the conclusion).
	Great Commemoration of Divine Being and work.
Sanctus (Isaiah vi. 3).	Sanctus.
Benedictus.	Benedictus.

WEST	EAST
CANON	
Te igitur (Prayer of oblation for the Church).	
Memento (Commemoration of the Living).	
Communicantes (Commemoration of the Saints).	
Hanc igitur (Prayer of oblation).	
Quam oblationem (Prayer for consecration).	Commemoration of Incarnation.
Qui pridie (Narrative of Institution).	Narrative of Institution.
Unde et memores ⎫ (Anamnesis Supra quae ⎬ and Supplices te ⎭ Oblation).	Anamnesis (memorial of Passion, Death, Resurrection, and Ascension) and Oblation.
Memento (Commemoration of the Dead).	Epiclesis.
Nobis quoque (Prayer for the Living, and Commemoration of Saints).	Oblation and Great Intercession.
Per quem (Conclusion, Consignation, i.e. signing with one species over the other, and Elevation).	
Paternoster, with prelude and embolism.	

III	III
	Litany.
	Lord's Prayer.
	Inclination and Elevation.
Fraction, Consignation, and Commixture.	Fraction and Commixture.
Agnus Dei.	*Koinonikon*, or Communion hymn.
Kiss of Peace.	

WEST	EAST
Communion.	Communion.
Ablutions.	
Oratio ad complendum (Post-Communion prayer).	Post-Communion hymn; Litany of Thanksgiving.
Ite, missa est.	Dismissal with blessing.
	———
	Distribution of antidoron.

The liturgy in the East continued to be performed with full ceremonial and with singing at all times; but in the West it became the custom, from the seventh century onwards, to use both the traditional form of Mass and also a simplified form, known as Low Mass, in which there was no singing and the priest, who was assisted only by a server, discharged the offices of deacon and subdeacon as well as that of celebrant.   From the eighth century it began to be the practice in the West to recite the Canon inaudibly, a novelty which owed more to the superstition of the age than to any advance on the reverence of the early Church.

Two novel practices in connexion with the use of the Sacrament were introduced during this period. Unleavened bread began to be used, probably as the result of a mistaken conclusion drawn by Charlemagne's scholars from their reading of the Gospels that the Last Supper was a Passover meal; and the method of administering the Bread by placing it in the communicant's mouth instead of in his hands

C.W.—7

seems to have originated in Gaul, where also women were forbidden to touch the chalice.

In the West the reserved Elements, in one kind or in both, were placed in a vessel called *Pyxis* or Pyx, which was kept in a cupboard (*armarium*, aumbry) in the wall of the sanctuary or in a hanging receptacle, frequently in the form of a dove, suspended over the altar. This was known as the *tabernaculum*. In the East the ἀρτοφόριον, as the receptacle was called, sometimes took the form of a model of a church and was placed upon the altar. Until the end of this period there was no devotional or other use of the reserved Elements apart from the single use of administration to communicants, sick or whole.

2. *The Daily Office.* Modifications of the Daily Office were effected in two ways during this period. In the middle of the eighth century the Office of the Saints, which had hitherto been used in the cemeteries outside the walls of Rome, began to be used in the basilicas in addition to the Daily Office on the appointed days. This resulted in the displacement of the ferial (ordinary) Office in some cases, with a consequent disturbance of the ordered sequence of psalms and lessons ; and in other cases it led to the performance of the Double Office, which involved a greater demand upon the time and devotion of those who sang it. Then in the early years of the

ninth century the liturgical reform instituted by Charlemagne effected a fusion of the Gallican and Roman methods of singing the Daily Office, and thus completed the work which Rome had herself begun for the reduction of the many divergences of local use.

For some years after the Carlovingian reform the secular clergy in Gaul and Germany omitted the singing of hymns in the Office, in order to conform to the use of Rome, which had not yet adopted them; but later they recovered the practice, which was never surrendered by the monks. Towards the end of the period it became the custom in some places to supplement the Daily Office with a set of Minor Offices, including the Office of the Blessed Virgin and the Office of the Dead. This indicates a changing theological outlook which was destined to work great changes in the Church's worship.

Grouping the various parts of the Daily Office according to their structure, and thus in all probability according to their separate origins in the early days of the Church's public worship, we find that Nocturns differs from all the others and is also the longest of the services; Lauds and Vespers are constructed on a common plan; Terce, Sext, and None are uniform; and Prime and Compline agree.

Nocturns began with introductory versicles and responses (prefaced at a later date by prayers said privately), as did all the divisions of the Office ; and then *Venite* (Psalm xcv.) was sung, preceded by an invitatory or antiphon, which was repeated at intervals. A variable hymn followed, and was succeeded by a single nocturn on weekdays and by three nocturns on Sundays. A nocturn includes :

(1) A group of psalms (twelve on ferial days, nine on festivals other than Sundays, and twelve, three, and three respectively in the Sunday nocturns) sung in weekly course from i. to cviii. (cix. in the English arrangement), omitting the 18 fixed psalms sung at the other Hours. Glorias and antiphons were interposed at regular intervals.

(2) Versicle, response, and Paternoster.

(3) A lesson read in three sections, each preceded by a benediction and followed by the chanting of a respond, which included :

(*a*) A response sung by the reader and repeated by the choir.

(*b*) A versicle sung by the reader, to which the choir replies with the second half of the response.

(*c*) The Gloria sung by the reader, and the full response sung by the choir.

On Sundays the lessons of the second and third nocturns were taken from the Fathers. All the other lessons came from the Scriptures. Isaiah was read during Advent; the other prophets from

Christmas to Sexagesima; the Pentateuch, Joshua, and Judges from Sexagesima to Holy Week; the Acts, the General Epistles, and the Apocalypse from Easter to Pentecost; Samuel, Kings, and Chronicles in the summer; and the Wisdom Books, with Esther, Judith, Esdras, and Maccabees, from the end of summer to December.

The service was brought to an abrupt conclusion by the recitation of a versicle and response; and on festivals this was prefaced by *Te Deum*.

Lauds and Vespers each provided five psalms to be sung immediately after the opening versicles and responses. At Lauds the first two of these varied according to the day of the week; the third was formed of Psalms lxii. and lxvi. (English lxiii. and lxvii.); the fourth was one of the seven Old Testament canticles; and the fifth was composed of the last three psalms in the Psalter sung continuously, from which the service took its name of Lauds. At Vespers the five psalms were sung in weekly course from cix. (cx.) to the end, omitting those that were included in the other Hours. At both services the psalms were followed by the reading of the Chapter (*capitulum*), which was preferably taken from the Epistle and usually consisted of only one verse. Then came a hymn, and after the hymn a canticle, *Benedictus* at Lauds and *Magnificat* at Vespers. The service was concluded by the Kyrie, the Paternoster, and the Preces (short intercessions), except on Sundays and Holydays, when, from the eighth century, the Collect of the Day took their place.

Terce, Sext, and None opened with the singing of a hymn after the introductory versicles and responses, each service having its own invariable hymn. Three sections of Psalm cxix., each consisting of sixteen verses, were then sung; the Chapter was read, and its short respond was chanted; and the service closed with the Kyrie and the Paternoster, or, after the eighth century, with the Collect of the Day on Sundays and other Holydays, as at Lauds and Vespers.

Prime and Compline have varied considerably in form in the course of their history; but the body of these two services consists of four fixed psalms and a Chapter with its respond. To this was added at Prime the Gallican use of *Quicunque vult* as an additional psalm; a fixed hymn was sung before the psalms; and at the end of the service there were added, from the eighth century, the Apostles' Creed, a form of confession and absolution, special Preces, and a special Collect. Compline also added a hymn (variable), the canticle *Nunc dimittis*, and the Apostles' Creed, etc., as for the conclusion of Prime: but these added elements appeared in different positions in the different parts of the Church.

3. *Litanies and Processions.* The inclusion of the

names of saints whose aid was sought by direct invocation is the chief characteristic of the litanies of this period. The names were commonly arranged in groups, as angels, apostles, martyrs, confessors, virgins, etc., the number of names in each group being uniform; and a litany was known in consequence as *trina, quina, septena,* and so on.

At the beginning of the ninth century the procession of palms on Palm Sunday, observed in Jerusalem as far back as the fourth century, was introduced in the West.

4. *Preaching and Teaching.* The general level of preaching in the parish churches during this period was very low. For the most part it was the work of an ignorant clergy addressing a still more ignorant laity; and the plainness of the manner of it was matched by the poverty of the matter. Texts were not commonly used, for there was little exposition of the Scriptures, and theology was neglected. Preachers busied themselves with miraculous stories of saints and images, especially with extravagant teaching about the Blessed Virgin, and with exhortation to the discharge of ecclesiastical duties. In the West sermons were usually delivered in the Latin tongue, but there was a growing tendency to preach in the vernacular; and in Gaul and Germany from the ninth century it became customary to add to the sermon at Mass a short office in the verna-

cular, called Prone. This gradually developed and came to include not only biddings to prayer, a general confession and absolution, and the giving out of notices, but also the teaching of the Creed, the Lord's Prayer, and the Ten Commandments, with instruction upon them.

Preaching in the monasteries reached a higher level, but it inevitably dealt largely with the monastic life. From the monasteries, however, went forth the missionaries, and their preaching among the heathen produced results which testify to its earnestness and power.

Of general preachers the greatest name in the East is that of the theologian St. John of Damascus (d. 754). In the West the most noteworthy were Rabanus Maurus (d. 856), a pupil of Alcuin; his fellow-student, Haymo (d. 853); Fulbert (d. 1029), who enjoyed a considerable reputation as a teacher among the Franks; and Ælfric (d. 1025), who is to be regarded as a founder of English preaching. Chief among the exponents of cloistral preaching were St. Theodore the Studite (d. 826) in the East, head of the famous Studion monastery at Constantinople, and the Saxon Bede (d. 735) and the Italian Peter Damiani (d. 1072) in the West. The greatest of the missionary preachers were the "apostle of Germany," St. Boniface (d. 755), the name by which Winfrid of Crediton is known, and

St. Anskar (*d.* 865), who laboured in Germany, Denmark, and Sweden.

VI.—THE HALLOWING OF LIFE

1. *Festivals and Fasts.* In the seventh century Septuagesima, Sexagesima, and Quinquagesima were set apart as Sundays leading to Lent, and Ash Wednesday and the three following days were included in the penitential season in order to give to it the full forty days which had been recommended in the Festal Letters of Athanasius as far back as 340. The use of ashes is found in association with the first day of Lent in the eighth century. By the end of the same century the Gallican observance of the three Rogation Days was established in Rome.

To the festivals of the Blessed Virgin there was added the feast of the Conception, which was first heard of in the East in the eighth century, appeared in the West in the tenth century, and became general in the twelfth century.

The commemoration of All Saints and All Souls, which had long been observed on various days in different localities, began to be generally kept on November 1 and 2 respectively towards the end of this period.

2. *Marriage.* Pope Nicholas I, writing in 866, supplies our first detailed account of Christian marriage. The solemn espousals (*sponsalia*), the

giving of a ring, and the executing of a marriage deed, preceded the nuptials (*nuptialia foedera*), which took place in church. The latter included the offering of oblations, the benediction of the man and woman, the veiling of the woman, the crowning of both, and the celebration of the nuptial Mass.

3. *Sickness and Death*. The monks cultivated herb gardens, maintained infirmaries, acquired some medical knowledge, and administered drugs and herbal remedies. But the Church still placed its trust mainly in prayer and sacramental healing ; and the people resorted to magical and superstitious practices. The gloom which had obscured the joy of the early Christian prospect of life after death was intensified by the retailing of dread visions of the other world. Prayers and Masses for the dead occupied a larger place in the religion of the people than hitherto ; the administration of the *viaticum* was regarded as an essential ministry to the dying ; and the burial of the dead took on a more sombre and penitential tone.

VII.—POPULAR DEVOTIONS

These continued as in the previous period, devotions to the Blessed Virgin growing in the popular estimation and consequently in their use.

CHAPTER IV

FROM THE ELEVENTH TO THE FOURTEENTH CENTURY

I.—A SURVEY OF THE PERIOD

The history of this period centres in the rise of the papacy to the height of its worldly power and in the decline which followed. During the three and a half centuries included within it the Bishops of Rome claimed the right to control completely the affairs of the Universal Church, and to direct to a large extent the affairs of every State in Christendom. Their claims were wholly rejected in the East, and they were frequently and vigorously opposed by the Empire and by the national groups which were growing into independent existence in the West. Yet it is true that, so far as Western Christendom is concerned, men's lives were dominated by the system in which the Western Church of that time expressed its conception of the Christian scheme of salvation; the Church itself held in men's minds the position of a supra-national State having divine authority; and the Pope was widely regarded as the supreme head of that State by the same authority and by imperial recognition of the fact.

After the death, in 1056, of the Emperor Henry

III, who had held the papacy largely in his power, a struggle began between the Bishops of Rome and the Hohenstaufen Emperors, in which the Church steadily gained ground. Of the series of able Popes who made this advance the most notable were Gregory VII (1073–1085) and Innocent III (1198–1216). The former, who is generally remembered as Hildebrand, accomplished the memorable humbling of Henry IV at Canossa in 1077. The latter raised the papacy to the very zenith of its worldly power. Forty years after the death of Henry III the crusading movement was initiated by Pope Urban II; and the long succession of crusades against the enemies of the Church—Turks in the East, and Albigenses and other heretics in the West—led to a great increase in the prestige of the Bishops of Rome, who not only advanced their leadership in Europe by this means, but also invaded the domain of the Eastern Church in Syria and Palestine, establishing Latin bishoprics there, and introducing the Latin rite. Further support for the papacy resulted from the founding of the orders of mendicant friars, who promoted a revival of religious fervour among the people in the thirteenth century, and stimulated loyalty to the Pope, under whose direct control they themselves served. Of the four orders that were established the Franciscans have a special importance in the history of worship for the part they played in the introduction of novel forms of popular devotion, and for the modification of the Church's official use which was effected by them, partly in order to meet the exigencies of their itinerant mode of life.

Early in the fourteenth century, however, a change came, and the papacy entered on evil days. France took it under control, as others had done before, but with the startling result that from 1309 to 1377 the Popes resided at Avignon, in Provence, suffering what is known as the Babylonish Captivity. Worse followed; for, when Gregory XI elected to return to Rome, a rival Pope was chosen, who maintained the Avignonese court over against the Roman, and thus began the Great Schism which lasted until 1417. This grave scandal in the Church was intensified by the knowledge of the existence of much worldliness and immorality among the secular clergy and members of the monastic orders; and not the splendour of the churches, nor the devotion of some of those who served them, nor even the spirituality of the numerous recluses and mystics of the age, could altogether deliver men's minds from the spirit of criticism or avail to check their growing hostility against ecclesiastical taxation and the commercialization of the Church's bestowal of the means of grace.

Meanwhile great changes had been taking place

in the world of thought and in the formulation of Christian dogma. Aristotle had been rediscovered by the Schoolmen, or Scholastic theologians, in the twelfth and thirteenth centuries ; and the master-mind of St. Thomas Aquinas had schematized the Faith with a thoroughness which seemed to leave nothing open to question and provided authoritative intellectual support for the all-inclusive claims of the medieval Church and for the full range of its developed sacramental usage. Outside the Church and its perfected theological system there was not only no salvation ; there was nothing of truth and nothing of value for the life of man. But the triumph of Scholasticism was as short-lived as the triumph of the papacy. The beginnings of modern literature and art and science were soon to make their appearance with disturbing effect ; and the challenges made by John Wyclif in England, by John Hus in Bohemia, and by Gerhard Groot in the Netherlands, heralded the storm which was to burst in the sixteenth century.

II.—ESTATES OF MEN AND THEIR FUNCTIONS IN WORSHIP

1. *The Laity.* Heresy and superstition appeared in many quarters during this period ; and there seems to have been a considerable amount of voluntary abstention from church-going in addition to

the disciplinary exclusion of large numbers of ex-communicate persons. Yet the vast majority of the people cared greatly for their parish churches, which they built and furnished with pious and generous zeal; their social life centred in them; they worshipped in them at the hour of Mattins and Mass on Sundays and Holydays, though ignorance of Latin and misconception of the nature of Christian priesthood constrained them to occupy themselves mainly with their own devotions; and they were all baptized and bishoped, shriven and communicated, married, churched, anointed, and buried by Holy Church, which continued to plead on their behalf long after they had passed away.

2. *The Clergy and their Assistants.* The wealth acquired by the Church through benefactions, and the immunity enjoyed by the clergy from various obligations resting upon the laity, led to a great dis-proportion in the number of men in orders, major and minor. It was not uncommon for as many as seven or eight hundred men to be admitted to one or other of the grades at one time in a diocese; and the result was seen in the idleness and im-morality of many who thus obtained exemption from their proper duties. As this period advanced, the bishops became increasingly unpopular in consequence of the exactions which they made in the interest of Rome; the average standard of

learning attained by the parish priests remained shamefully inadequate; and the specific functions of the deacons were taken away from them by the withdrawal of the chalice from the laity on the one hand and by the social work of the friars on the other, so that the diaconate practically lapsed. Towards the end of the twelfth century, in the interests of celibacy, the subdiaconate began to be incorrectly reckoned, in the West, as one of the major orders, which were thus restored to the original number of three, having been diminished in the fifth century by the denial that the episcopate is an order distinct from the priesthood.

In 1095 it was decreed by the Council of Placentia that general ordinations should be held at the Ember seasons, a practice which dates back to at least the seventh century in England as at Rome; and from that time onwards the original significance of Embertide was gradually lost sight of. At the ordination of priests and the consecration of bishops *Veni Creator* was sung, and the tradition of the paten and chalice to priests was now accompanied by the words " Receive power to offer sacrifice to God, and to celebrate Mass both for the living and the dead." Immediately before the concluding Collect of the Mass the laying on of hands was repeated, with the words " Receive the Holy Ghost. Whose sins thou dost forgive, they are forgiven; and whose sins thou dost retain, they are retained." These changes stereotyped a distorted conception of priesthood.

The bishop's mitre assumed its familiar shape during this period, and, in growing gradually taller, suggested already the distorted form of later days; and the rochet came into use as a distinctively episcopal habit, in the form of a linen alb without girdle, worn both in and out of church. The alb proper was decorated, from the eleventh century, with ornamental borders running round the wrists and the hems of the garment; and these were presently reduced to short pieces (apparels) applied to the front and back of the hem and to the back of the wrists. The chasuble commonly bore the Y-cross, or orphrey, from the twelfth century onwards. In the same century the surplice (*superpelliceum*, i.e. garment worn over the pelisse) came into use as a choir habit, displacing the alb which could not conveniently be worn over the fur-lined gown necessitated by cold churches. In the thirteenth century dignitaries began to wear a cape or strip of fur, called an almuce, over the head or on the shoulders; and in the course of the following three centuries this assumed the form of a cape with two ends hanging down in front, and also of a mere scarf. The hood was worn as a head-covering by clerics and monks as well as by lay-people, its *liripipium*, or pocket, which hung down from the back of it, being sometimes coiled round the neck, and developing subsequently into the tippet or scarf.

3. *The Religious Orders*. In the middle of the eleventh century the Augustinian or Austin Canons, priests living the monastic life, were included among the monastic orders. In 1086 the severely ascetic Carthusian Order was established. In 1098 the Cistercian Order was founded at Cîteaux in Burgundy for the stricter observance of the Benedictine Rule ; and, largely as a result of the cessation of the raids of the Northmen, there was a great revival in the monastic life in the twelfth century. In the first half of the thirteenth century came the new movement of the Friars, Franciscan, Dominican, Austin, and Carmelite, who were popular with the people wherever they went, as friends of the poor, as preachers and confessors, and as instructors in homely devotions. Monks, canons, nuns, and friars together sustained the chief part of the Church's obligation to worship, practised agriculture and various industries, performed valuable social services by their ministrations to the poor, promoted learning and literature, and assisted in the development of music, architecture, and art. The evils that are so readily detected in their lives during the recurring periods of declension from the ideals which first gave birth to their Orders ought not to

blind us to the strenuousness of their practice of worship and the value of the services which they rendered in conjunction with it.

III.—PLACES OF WORSHIP; AND LITURGICAL BOOKS AND MUSIC

1. *Places of Worship.* Byzantine church architecture showed no important development after the eighth century. In the West, on the contrary, there was a constant growth. During this period the heavy Romanesque style of building developed until the first half of the twelfth century, and was then transformed into the lighter and more graceful style known as Gothic, which reached its perfection by the middle of the fourteenth century. This evolution of architectural style, which was accomplished most notably in northern and central France, represents essentially an increasing mastery in the art of stone-vaulting, a mastery recorded in the pointed arch, the slender, elaborated pillar, and the enlarged window.

In England there was at first much building of castles and monasteries after the Norman Conquest; and the beginning of the twelfth century saw a remarkable outbreak of church-building, in the Norman Romanesque style, all over the country. In many of these new churches the apse was substituted for the familiar rectangular east end; the west front, which was pierced by the chief entrance to the church, was frequently elaborated; and the central tower became common, even where the cruciform plan was not adopted. The round churches which were built by the Templars and Hospitallers were copied from the Church of the Holy Sepulchre at Jerusalem and were a result of the Crusades.

The Gothic development, which dates from the second half of the twelfth century, passed through two stages, generally characterized as Early English (1175–1245) and Decorated (1245–1348), before building was checked by the coming of the Black Death; or, if reference be made to the changing styles of window-tracery, it passed through three stages, which are described as Lancet (1175–1245), Geometrical (1245–1315), and Curvilinear (1315–1348). The ground plan of the majority of the churches built at this time was the longitudinal, consisting of nave and chancel, with added aisles in which additional altars were placed; the rectangular east end was usually restored; the main entrance was placed on the south side, and a porch, generally containing a holy-water stoup, was built outside it, for use at churchings and the introductory parts of the baptismal and marriage services; and spires were built on many of the towers, which were usually erected at the west end, except in the case of

the larger churches.   Between the chancel and the
nave there was a screen which carried the rood with
its attendant figures of the Virgin and St. John and
a platform or gallery for singers.   Against the east
wall stood the altar, now almost invariably made of
stone, though wooden altars had persisted until the
eleventh century ; and frequently now it bore a
cross and one candle or two.   On the south side of
the sanctuary were *sedilia* (seats) for the use of the
three sacred ministers at Mass, and a *piscina* (sink)
for the washing of the priests' hands and of the
Communion vessels.   The interiors of the churches
were made colourful, and at the same time instruc-
tive, by means of painted windows, frescoes, and
hangings.   The pulpit was commonly a small movable structure.   Stone seats set against the walls for
the use of the infirm were as a rule the only seats
provided ; and the floors, which were of earth or
stone, the chancels sometimes being tiled, were
periodically strewn with rushes, straw, box, and
fragrant leaves.

   2. *Liturgical Books and Music.*   For the convenience of priests at Low Mass the various parts of the
service were gathered into a single book, called the
Missal, in the eleventh century ; and similarly the
material required for the recitation of the Daily
Office was brought together in a book called the
Breviary (abridgment) or Portiforium (carried

abroad)—in England, Portos or Portuis—for the use of those who recited the Office privately or when travelling. In the thirteenth century the Processional, or litany-book, was compiled from the Antiphonary and the Responsorial. The production of copies of the separate books from which these three were compiled did not cease, however, throughout the Middle Ages. The contents of the composite books were usually arranged so as to give the invariable parts of the service in the middle; while the variable parts which preceded and followed this fixed section included the *Temporale*, or *proprium de tempore*, which provided for the observance of the changing seasons of the Church's Year, the *Sanctorale*, or *proprium de sanctis*, which provided for the observance of particular Holydays, and the *Commune sanctorum*, which provided for groups of Saints' Days.

From the Sacramentary the various forms of consecration and blessing used by the bishop were now brought together in a book called the Pontifical; and, in the fourteenth century, the forms required by the parish priest were brought together in a book called the Manual or Ritual. For guidance in the conduct of services the *Ordinale* and the *Consuetudinarium* were provided.

While the forms of service in use in the cathedral and parish churches throughout the West were now to a large extent uniform, there remained a measure of divergence in details, according to diocesan use as authorized by the bishop in the exercise of his *jus liturgicum*. The Use of Sarum (Salisbury) was increasingly adopted in other English dioceses.

Two books containing music for the Mass were known as the *Graduale* or *Gradale* (in English Grayle or Grail) and the *Troperium* (in English Troper). The former, which was the *Antiphonarium* of former days, provided music for the scriptural passages sung during Mass, viz. :

(1) *Antiphona ad introitum* (called *Officium* in the Sarum Missal).

(2) *Graduale* (sung between Epistle and Gospel), followed by *Alleluia*, or by *Tractus* at certain penitential and funeral Masses (sung *tractim*, or continuously, by the cantor).

(3) *Offertorium*, which, with the decay of the Offertory, had lost its verses.

(4) *Antiphona ad communionem*, with its psalm.

The second book, the Troper, was so called from the *tropi* (" turns ") of the words and music it contained, which were farsed or interpolated in certain non-scriptural passages sung during Mass, viz. : *Kyrie*, *Gloria in excelsis*, *Sanctus*, and *Agnus Dei*. The *Sequentia* (Sequence), or *Prosa* (Prose), which was also found in the Troper, took its name from the deacon's announcement of the Gospel—

" *Sequentia evangelii secundum, etc.*," and consisted of *prosa ad sequentiam*, or words fitted to the *Jubilus* (the long-drawn-out final syllable of the *Alleluia*), which was made to last until the deacon's procession had arrived at the *ambo* or *pulpitum* for the Gospel.

The advance from singing in unison to singing in parts, which was begun by the introduction of the *organum*, was carried a stage farther by the use of the descant, an independent melody sung above the true melody with some freedom of movement. From this developed the use of counterpoint with such liberty of musical embellishment that ecclesiastical authority, moved by fear of the obscuring of the words sung, ordered a reversion to the use of the *organum*. The development of polyphony could not be prevented, however; and a way was presently found, through the use of the *faux-bourdon*, which gave the melody to the tenor voices (" false tenor ") while accompaniment was made by the other voices. Musical notation was advanced by the substitution of black notes indicating exact intervals and time-values for the neumes which had hitherto been used; and the descantists brought in the use of red notes to signify the loss of a proportion of their value. In the fourteenth century the notation in open notes began to displace both the black and red notes.

IV.—INITIATION AND ECCLESIASTICAL DISCIPLINE

1. *Initiation.*   The first part of the sacrament of initiation was administered to infants as soon as possible after birth, except that any who were born within eight days of Easter or of Pentecost waited for the solemn celebration of the sacrament on the eve of the festival.   The Sarum rite falls into four parts.

(1) *Ordo ad faciendum catechumenum* (Order for Making a Catechumen).   This introduction corresponded closely with the ancient form in all but the exsufflation and the instruction, which were omitted. The priest met the godparents and the child at the church door and, after questioning them as to the child's sex, unbaptized condition, and name, he prayed, signed the child's forehead with the sign of the cross, placed salt in its mouth, pronounced the exorcisms, read from St. Matthew the account of our Lord's blessing the children, performed the Effeta with saliva, and recited with the godparents and friends the Paternoster, Ave, and Credo.   Then he signed the child's right hand with the sign of the cross, and taking hold of the hand led the procession into the church and to the font.

(2) *Benedictio fontis* (Benediction of the Font). This was an independent rite, not performed on each occasion of baptizing, but only on the eves

of Easter and Pentecost and at intervals subsequently, when it became necessary to change the water in the font, which was kept closed and sealed. It consisted of a litany and a long prayer in the manner of the Preface at Mass; and during the recitation of the prayer the priest made the sign of the cross in the water with his right hand, he scattered water from the font in four directions, he breathed upon it three times in the form of a cross, he dropped into it wax from a candle in the form of a cross, he divided it crosswise with the candle, and finally he poured in oil and chrism in the form of a cross.

(3) *Ritus baptizandi* (Rite of Baptizing). Having asked once more the name of the child and having obtained from the godparents the vow of renunciation of evil, the priest anointed the child on the breast and between the shoulders. He then questioned the sponsors as to faith in the Creed and desire for Baptism, and proceeded to baptize the swaddled child by triple immersion, with its head to the east each time, and its face to the north, south, and to the water, in turn. The godparents then received the child from the priest, who anointed the crown of his head with chrism, put upon him a white robe known as the chrisom, and placed a lighted taper in his hand.

(4) *Confirmatio puerorum* (Confirmation of Chil-

dren).   On the rare occasions when the bishop was
present he proceeded at once to complete the child's
initiation by administering Confirmation.   Normally, however, it was after an interval, which during
the Middle Ages tended to increase to seven years,
that the brief rite was performed by the bishop
on his visitation tour either in church or in the
open, to suit his convenience.   After versicles
and a prayer for the sevenfold gift of the Spirit,
the bishop signed the candidates on the forehead
with chrism, but was no longer required to lay
on his hand.   A prayer and a blessing concluded
the rite.

2. *Ecclesiastical Discipline.*   In 1215 the Fourth
Council of the Lateran made compulsory that practice of private confession which had spread from
the monasteries to the outer world and had been
increasingly adopted in the parishes.   At least once
a year every Christian who had reached years of discretion must now confess his sins with all fidelity to
his own priest.   To meet the frequent objections
that were raised to this restriction permission was
given subsequently to resort to another priest with
the consent of the priest to whom jurisdiction
rightly belonged.   The friars began to monopolize
the Confessional under papal authority and to rival
the parish priests.

The sacramental theory of absolution which had

developed during the twelfth century was formulated with precision by the Schoolmen in the thirteenth century. Sins were either venial or mortal; and in the latter case it was necessary that confession should be made to the Church, which could ensure divine forgiveness by applying sacramental grace for the conversion of the attrition, or imperfect penitence, of the sinner into contrition, or true penitence. The " matter " of the sacrament was defined as consisting of the contrition of the penitent, his confession, and the satisfaction (penance) performed by him at the Church's bidding. The " form " of the sacrament was the declaratory absolution *Ego te absolvo*, which in the thirteenth century displaced the precatory absolution that had hitherto been generally used. Outside the use of private confession the *Confiteor*, or form of confession used by the penitent, began to be said at the altar by the priest and ministers before Mass in the thirteenth century, and it was used also at Prime and Compline; but on these occasions the precatory form of absolution was retained.

The practice of remitting a part of appointed penances by indulgences was extended to complete remission, or plenary indulgence, for the first time in 1095, when it was decreed at the Council of Clermont that crusaders should be thus privileged. Pilgrimages, services rendered to the Church, and particularly the payment of money, were increasingly accepted as grounds for the commutation of penance in part or in full.

Public penance for crimes and moral offences, for ecclesiastical offences such as non-attendance at church, and for heresy, which was sought out by means of the inquisition established by Innocent III in 1215, took the form of whipping, fines, imprisonment, and excommunication.   The last of these was of two grades, lesser and greater, the anathema becoming equivalent to the latter in the twelfth century.   This excluded offenders from public worship and the offices of the Church and forbade their burial in consecrated ground.   An interdict was a papal prohibition which extended the same penalties to a whole community or to a particular territory.

V.—CORPORATE WORSHIP

1. *The Eucharist.*   During this period the Eucharist in the West arrived at length at the stage, regarded by some as a true development and by others as a corrupt transformation, which is commonly implied by the modern use of the term Mass. The rite itself underwent but little change, the few additions that were made to it proceeding mainly from a desire to emphasize and explain certain gestures.   Eucharistic theology, on the contrary, advanced to the settlement of debated questions and

to the conclusion of a long-continued process of developing opinion by the formulation of exact interpretations of the essential mystery and primary use of the sacrament ; and in ceremonial, administration, and extra-liturgical use, novelties of a highly significant character were introduced.

As far back as the ninth century Paschasius Radbertus had taught that after consecration there exists in the Elements nothing but the Body and Blood of Christ. Although this opinion was confuted by Rabanus Maurus and Ratramnus, it commended itself widely ; and being held by very many in the eleventh century it was challenged again by Berengarius of Tours. Berengarius, however, yielded to ecclesiastical pressure ; gross views of the nature of the presence of Christ in the sacrament were encouraged and yet more widely held ; and the philosophic subtleties of the doctrine of Transubstantiation, which was formulated by the Schoolmen for the correction of materialistic views and adopted by the Fourth Council of the Lateran in 1215, availed in the popular mind only to cover its own errors with authority. In close connexion with the doctrine of the effect of eucharistic consecration there developed the doctrine of the virtue of the eucharistic sacrifice ; and though the theologians of the period arrived at no such exact definition of the latter doctrine as they had achieved in the ormer, the doctrine of Transubstantiation sufficed to encourage the growth of the popular idea of the Mass as a repeated presentation of the material Body and Blood and consequently as a repetition of the prevailing sacrifice made upon the Cross, committed to the power of the Church, and of unlimited efficacy in the matters to which the Church applied it.

The practical outcome of this was the multiplication of Masses for the benefit of the living and the dead. It became a general rule for all priests to say Mass daily, and numerous chapels and altars were provided in the larger churches in order to meet their need. But in the parish churches the Mass was not normally for Communion but for sacrifice and adoration. While priests necessarily communicated every time they celebrated, and monks and nuns and friars were accustomed to receive Communion frequently, very infrequent Communion, generally only once a year, became the accepted standard of the laity. Lay people attended Mass on Sundays and Holydays ; lords and ladies might hear Mass daily in their own chapels ; but their primary object was to witness the miracle of Transubstantiation, as they understood it, to adore the Christ whose presence was thus effected, and to win the benefits of His sacrifice accomplished anew by the priest at the altar, more especially on behalf of the souls in purgatory. In order to focus and stimulate the adoration of the Faithful, and also, as some would have it, in order to proclaim that the consecration of the bread was effected independently of the consecration of the wine, the practice of elevating the Host above the priest's head immediately after consecration was adopted in the thirteenth century, attention being called to this by the ringing of a bell before and after consecration. This " greater elevation " as a manward demonstration, in place of the customary elevation in token of a Godward offering, was extended to the chalice in the fourteenth century. It was natural that the adoration thus invited and practised in the course of the Mass itself should be extended to the Elements reserved ; and this duly followed.

Early in the twelfth century the chalice began to be withheld from all but the celebrant of each Mass ; and in spite of much opposition this serious departure from our Lord's express command and the hitherto unbroken practice of the Church was widely adopted in the course of the next few centuries and was duly authorized in the fifteenth century. The kiss of peace was given at this time to a paten or other sacred object made to serve as an *osculatorium*, most commonly a tablet of ivory or of embossed metal on wood, called a pax or pax-brede (pax-board). This was passed round the congregation in order according to their rank.

2. *The Daily Office*. In the twelfth century a revised and abbreviated form of the Daily Office was taken into use in the Papal Chapel at Rome. This new *Breviarium Romanae Curiae* shortened the passages to be read from the Scriptures ; it added to the number of the festivals to be observed and attached octaves to some of them ; it authorized the use of the hymns which were sung in the monastic rendering of the Daily Office ; and it introduced the Office of the Blessed Virgin Mary, the Office of the Dead, and certain memorials, to be recited as supplementary forms. The Franciscans, who adopted this *Modernum Officium* for their own use, obtained permission from Pope Gregory IX to revise it again, and in 1241 a revision made by their general, Haymo of Faversham, was approved. This second revision reduced still further the length of the scriptural lections ; it added many more saints' days and introduced the practice of observing octaves of feasts on each of the following seven days instead of on the last of them only ; it imported much legendary matter to be read as Saints' Days lessons ; and it provided for the recitation of the *Paternoster* before and after each canonical Office and of the *Ave Maria* before and after each Office of the Blessed Virgin, and for the singing of four anthems of the Blessed Virgin at Compline. This Franciscan revision of the Breviary was adopted by the Papal Curia ; and

the Franciscan Pope Nicholas III secured its use in the churches of Rome. The friars themselves popularized it throughout Western Europe; and in England it became the model of the various diocesan forms of the Daily Office, including that of Sarum.

In the monasteries of the different Orders the Daily Office was sung at varying intervals in the course of the twenty-four hours. Nocturns and Lauds were combined for the night-office at some hour of the night or very early morning; and at this time the title Mattins, which strictly belonged to Lauds, was applied to the combined Office and presently to Nocturns alone. The day-hours of Prime, Terce, Sext, and None were everywhere sung at the proper hours. Vespers and Compline were sung in the evening, and were usually divided by supper and a reading, called collation, from some ascetic author. The Chapter Mass preceded Terce in the winter and followed it in the summer. High Mass was sung immediately before Sext.

The parochial clergy recited the Office in three, or two, groups, a common arrangement being the saying of Mattins and Lauds overnight, the day-hours in one group in the morning, and Vespers and Compline soon after midday. The laity as a rule regarded the Office as no concern of theirs, except on Sundays.

3. *Litanies and Processions*. Great use was made

of processions in the worship of the medieval Church, the degree of pageantry displayed, the routes taken, the " stations " or halts made for prayer, and the choice of responds and antiphons, proses and hymns, psalms and litanies, sung on the way, varying according to the occasion. Thus there was a procession in church before Mass every Sunday and on certain Holydays, and frequently also a procession of a different character at Vespers on the preceding evening, when the service was led to some altar or to the Rood, and special prayers were said there. Wednesdays and Fridays in Lent were marked by a similar procession. On Palm Sunday, Ascension Day, and the feast of Corpus Christi, the procession left the church, and returned to it again after making its way through the surrounding churchyard. And on the Rogation Days and St. Mark's Day it was the custom to go farther afield, through the streets and the open country.

4. *Preaching and Teaching.* At the parish Mass on Sundays and Holydays the clergy were required to preach on the Gospel appointed for the day, or to give instruction on the Creed, the Commandments, the Sacraments, the Seven Virtues and the Seven Deadly Sins, and such matters. For this duty it is to be feared that many of them were very ill-equipped. Poor preaching and foolish preaching were still widely prevalent during this period.

Many preachers were dependent upon the material
provided in the Homiliaries; many trusted to
labour-saving compilations, such as the *Speculum
Ecclesiae* of the German Honorius Scholasticus (*d.*
1150) and the *Deflorationes Patrum* of his fellow-
countryman Werner of Ellerbach (*d.* 1126); and
the continuing fondness for unedifying fables, alle-
gories, and parables, is attested by the great popularity of a collection of these in verse by Walter de
Mapes, chaplain to Henry II. But there was on the
whole an improvement in preaching power, if not
in the material of the sermons preached; and the
age produced a considerable number of really great
preachers in the West. The chief factors contribut-
ing to this recovery were the stimulus presented by
the spread of heresy, the intellectual quickening
resulting from contact with the Saracens, and the
growth of vernacular languages.

The Crusades were begun under the influence of
the preaching of Urban II (*d.* 1099), a Frenchman
who had been a monk at Cluny, of Peter the Hermit
(*d.* 1115), and of St. Bernard of Clairvaux (*d.* 1153),
the mystic, the unflinching opponent of Peter
Abailard, and the greatest preacher of the twelfth
century. In the thirteenth century came the
preaching friars. Heretical movements, in particular the heresy of the Albigenses in southern
France, were met by the preaching of the Domini-

cans, who laid strong intellectual foundations for their work ; and the Faithful, especially the common folk, were everywhere stimulated by the evangelistic fervour and popular preaching of the Franciscans, who freely used their imagination in presenting their message, and cultivated a telling simplicity of style. Two of the greatest of the Franciscan preachers were St. Antony of Padua (*d.* 1231), a Portuguese who laboured in France and Italy, and Berthold of Regensburg (Ratisbon) in Bavaria (*d.* 1272), an evangelist of remarkable popularity.

The Schoolmen and the Mystics of the period made characteristic contributions to its preaching, and furnished preachers of a high order, such as Albertus Magnus (*d.* 1280), a Dominican of South Germany, and his greatest pupil, St. Thomas Aquinas (*d.* 1274), a member of the same Order, and, among the exponents of mystical and devotional preaching, the Franciscan Bonaventura (*d.* 1274), the Dominican Eckhart (*d.* 1327), his pupil the ascetic Henry Suso (*d.* 1366), and, greatest of all, the Dominican, John Tauler (*d.* 1361). By the fourteenth century, however, there was again a marked deterioration in the general standard of preaching, and the noble preaching of the great Schoolmen had given place to exhibitions of intellectual dexterity in the discussion of subjects remote from Christian life and practice, such as " Whether God could sin if He chose."

VI.—THE HALLOWING OF LIFE

1. *Festivals and Fasts*. The feast of Corpus Christi, in honour of the Sacrament of the Altar, was instituted by Pope Urban IV in 1264 and was appointed to be observed on the Thursday after Trinity Sunday, that being the first " free " Thursday after Maundy Thursday, the day of the institution of the Sacrament. Trinity Sunday itself, though it had begun to be observed in the tenth century, was not generally kept until 1334, when its observance was ordered by Pope John XXII. In the Eastern Church the Sundays after Whitsunday were mostly named after the Gospel appointed for the day. In the West they were variously numbered—after Whitsunday in Rome and in France, after Trinity Sunday in many parts of Germany, Scandinavia, and England, notably according to the Sarum Use, and after the octave of Trinity Sunday by the Dominicans.

In 1389 Pope Urban VI instituted the feast of the Visitation of the Blessed Virgin Mary, which was confirmed by the Council of Basle (1431–1449).

There was as yet nothing in the nature of accepted sequences of colour in the hangings and vestments to mark the different seasons and festivals ; but there are signs of the beginnings of system in the practice of various important churches and of a growing agreement as to the suitability of white or cream, of reds of all sorts, of mixed white and red, of greens and yellows of many shades, and of black, blue, purple, russet, or grey, for particular occasions.

2. *Marriage and Childbirth*.   The customary form of the marriage service continued unchanged, its details in England, according to the Sarum Manual, being as follows.   Banns were read in the vernacular at Mass on three separate Sundays or Holydays, consecutive days not being allowed. The espousals, or first part of the service, took place at the church door.   The questions put by the priest and the vows taken by the contracting parties were said in English ; gold and silver were laid on the priest's book together with the ring ; and the ring was blessed, sprinkled with holy water, and placed in turn on the first, second, and third fingers of the bride's right hand, in the Name of the three Persons of the Trinity in order, and on the fourth finger, where it remained, to the word *Amen*. The whole party then entered the church and followed the priest towards the altar, reciting Psalm cxxviii. Prayers were said at the altar step ; and, when the bridal pair had taken their place on the south side of the presbytery, Mass was begun. A formal blessing upon the marriage was pronounced immediately before the act of Communion.

The Office for the Churching of Women, which

was included in the Sarum Manual under the title *Purificatio post Partum*, provided for the recitation of Psalms cxxi. and cxxviii. at the church door, followed by the *Kyrie*, the *Paternoster*, versicles, and prayer; and, after being sprinkled with holy water, the woman was received into church with the words, "Enter into the temple of God that thou mayest have eternal life and live for ever."

3. *Sickness and Death*. The Offices for the visitation of the sick, for the commendation of the soul at the time of death, and for the burial of the dead, were contained in the Manual, together with the necessary forms for the administration of unction and of the Holy Communion. According to the Sarum Manual the priest recited the seven Penitential Psalms on his way to the sick man's house. When he arrived he pronounced an invocation of peace upon it, proceeded to the sick-room, and there said the *Kyrie*, the *Paternoster*, versicles, and prayers. After an exhortation to patience and faith and a brief examination in the Creed there was another exhortation to charity and hope, and yet a third to contrition and confession. When the sick man's confession had been heard, the priest closed the Office with a Collect and the blessing.

The anointing of the sick had by this time become, in the West, "extreme unction" or *unctio in extremis*; and, though the original idea of anointing with a view to healing was not altogether lost, this unction of the organs of the senses, the feet, and the loins, was generally reserved for the dying and was held to be for the remission of sins. The anointing was followed by the administration of the *viaticum*.   The Office for the commendation of a soul at the hour of death included a litany, a commendation beginning *Proficiscere anima christiana* (Set forth, O Christian soul), and short suffrages.

The Office for the burial of the dead was preceded, in the Sarum Manual, by a collection of psalms and prayers, known as *Commendatio animarum*, to be recited on the day of death, or on the eve of the burial during the preparation of the body for removal to the church.   Vespers, Compline, and the Vigils of the Dead (*Placebo* and *Dirige*) were then said ; the funeral Mass was celebrated ; and the burial service followed.   Antiphons, Kyries, and prayers were said in church, the priest censing the body and sprinkling it with holy water.   Psalms were sung during the procession to the grave ; and after the grave had been blessed and censed the body was laid in it, numerous prayers followed with psalms interspersed, earth was thrown on the body in the form of a cross, and the priest again commended the soul to God.   After more prayers and psalms the procession returned to the church singing one or more of the Penitential Psalms.   The effect of the Office as a whole was to invest death with gloom and the future with apprehension. The pains of Purgatory, so vividly suggested by the pictures in church windows and the paintings on church walls, were uppermost in the minds of the mourners; and the general effect produced by the funeral was intensified by the repetition of the Mass and the Vigils of the Dead on the third, seventh, and thirtieth days afterwards.

VII.—POPULAR DEVOTIONS

The medieval Guilds of craftsmen and others had their patron saints, their own chapels and churches where Guild Masses were said and where the festivals of their saints were specially observed, their processions in honour of the saints, and their Trade or Mistery Plays setting forth the story of their lives and miraculous deeds. Relics of the saints were on sale in great quantities as a result of the Crusades; and churches which acquired them by purchase or by the good fortune of a more direct association became centres of pilgrimage and receivers of the offerings brought by the pilgrims.

The frequent repetition of the *Ave Maria* was widely practised as a form of devotion by the thirteenth century; and many people used this and other forms, with abstinence or fasting on certain days, in the belief that the Blessed Virgin would secure for them special rewards. The *Angelus*, which was introduced in the thirteenth century, to be said at the ringing of the church bell in the morning, at noon, and in the evening, was essentially a memorial of the Annunciation, and became a devotion to the Blessed Virgin. The rosary came into use in connexion with the practice, adopted by illiterate monks, of reciting fifty, a hundred, or a hundred and fifty, Paternosters in place of the hundred and fifty psalms which others said for the dead; and from the thirteenth century the *Ave Maria* began to be used in this way in place of the *Paternoster*.

The prayer-book of the laity was the *Horae* (Book of Hours), which was made to serve for instruction as well as devotion, and came to be called the Prymer. The contents of these books varied greatly, but they generally included the Hours of the Blessed Virgin, the Vigils of the Dead and the Commendation, the Penitential and the Gradual Psalms, and a litany.

The introduction of the Christmas Crib and the Stations of the Cross was due to Franciscan influence, and is to be connected with the gradual development of the dramatic element in the Liturgy, which issued in the presentation of Mystery and Miracle Plays in church and churchyard.

CHAPTER V

THE RENAISSANCE AND THE CONTINENTAL REFORMATION

I.—A SURVEY OF THE PERIOD

The transition from the Middle Ages to the Modern Age was effected by the Renaissance, or re-birth of the mind of southern and western Europe ; by the emergence of strong monarchies in comple-tion of the process of nation-building which had been taking place since the dissolution of the Roman Empire ; by geographical discoveries which greatly enlarged the intellectual and political hori-zons of men's minds ; and by the Reformation of the Church's system of doctrine and practice in a large part of western Christendom, and its final and absolute repudiation of the authority of the Bishop of Rome.

The Renaissance, which is to be traced to the contact with Greek and Saracen learning estab-lished by the Crusades in the East and by the Moors in Spain, was markedly affecting the culture of certain Italian cities by the middle of the fourteenth century. There it took the form of a creative enthusiasm for literature and art, which fed upon classical antiquity, produced its own great works in remarkable abundance, and propagated a spirit which fostered both sensuality and scepticism. It spread to France in the course of the next hundred years, and, towards the end of that time, to the Netherlands, Germany, and England, concerning itself with learning, and particularly with the Greek New Testament, in these three countries more seriously than elsewhere. In Italy it received a great stimulus from the advent of refugee Greek scholars, as a result of the capture of Constantinople by the Turks in 1453. Printing was invented in 1455; and in 1543 Copernicus pronounced that the sun, not the earth, was the centre of our planetary system. In all this there was obviously much that involved men in the necessity of re-thinking and re-stating the content of Christian truth, and not a little that countenanced departure from the moral discipline of the Church and thus prepared, in turn, for a revolt against ecclesiastical authority that condoned and practised grave laxity of conduct.

In the sixteenth century the leading nation was Spain, which had united Aragon with Castile in 1469, driven the Moors out of Granada in 1492, and added to herself Naples and Sicily, the Netherlands, and the Empire, under Charles V, in 1519. France, having expelled the English from her territories at the conclusion of the Hundred Years' War, was raised to the position of a great State by Louis XI, who died in 1483. England was strongly ruled by the Tudors, who responded wisely to the needs and the opportunity created by the Wars of the Roses. Switzerland had established anew against Charles, Duke of Burgundy, the independence it had won from Austria in 1386. And the Empire, after suffering a prolonged period of disorder in the fifteenth century and being united with Spain in 1519, renewed its separate existence in 1556. The problem of combining national independence in a number of powerful States with loyalty to a supra-national Church which laid claim to more than spiritual authority was thus presented in an acute form.

In the latter half of the fifteenth century adventurers from Spain and Portugal, and from Italy and England, set sail across the seas on successful voyages which not only added to men's knowledge of the world and brought pledges of great increase of riches, but by so doing stimulated national loyalty and intensified national self-consciousness and the spirit of international competition far more than they promoted the cause of unity in the Church to which all belonged, though considerations of missionary endeavour were not lacking.

Thus the time was fully ripe for an attempt to correct the many evils attaching to the ecclesiastical system of the Middle Ages; and it was to be expected that it would take place on national lines in a

variety of forms determined by the political conditions and the general ethos of each of the groups
concerned.   Councils of the Western Church had
met at Pisa in 1409, at Constance in 1414, at
Basle in 1431, and at Florence in 1439, with very
inadequate results. Savonarola had embarked on
a vigorous reform of morals in Italy itself, but
had been burnt at the stake in 1498.   When,
however, Martin Luther at Wittenberg boldly
denounced the sale of indulgences, in 1517, thinking
to persuade the Church to the correction of an
obvious and grievous fault, the accumulated forces
of critical and reforming zeal carried him onward
in a tempestuous movement which raged violently
over the whole of western Christendom and ruthlessly tore it asunder.   The patriot Zwingli initiated
a parallel but independent protest in German
Switzerland at Zürich in 1522, while from Geneva
the Frenchman, Calvin, who had fled from his
own country, led the reformation of the Church
in French Switzerland between the years 1541 and
1564, and absorbed the work of Zwingli, who had
died a soldier's death in 1531.   Luther and Calvin
divided between them the allegiance of all Protestant
Christendom on the Continent. Lutheranism established itself so rapidly and so strongly in the States
of the Empire that in 1558 it was computed that
only a tenth part of the people remained Catholic ;

and even before that date it had become dominant in Denmark, Norway, Sweden, and Iceland, while it triumphed, and then was held in check, in Poland, Bohemia, Hungary, and Transylvania. Calvinism secured for itself a strong position in Switzerland, its original home, in France, where the name Huguenots was applied to the Protestants, and in the Netherlands though not in Belgium. It also made its way into the German States, where Calvinists came to be known as the Reformed, a term which stands generally for Calvinist as opposed to Lutheran.

The Eastern Church maintained itself during these years under peculiar difficulties. After the capture of Constantinople in 1453 the Turks possessed themselves of a large part of south-eastern Europe, and the Holy Orthodox Church was thus severed in two, one section being permitted to exist under Turkish rule, while the other remained under the control of Russia, which had been converted to Christianity in the latter half of the ninth century. Both parts looked to the Patriarch of Constantinople as their chief bishop until, in 1589, an independent patriarchate was established at Moscow.

II.—ESTATES OF MEN AND THEIR FUNCTIONS IN WORSHIP

1. *The Laity.* The Continental Reformation repudiated the sacrifice of the Mass, abolished the

ministerial priesthood, and asserted the evangelical doctrine of the priesthood of the laity in terms of the right to a first-hand knowledge and use of the Bible, to an unmediated approach to the throne of mercy, and to an active share in the Church's public worship. In its insistence upon congregational worship, rendered in the people's tongue and contributed to by all, it was clearly returning to the practice of the primitive Church ; but where it subordinated eucharistic worship to services of psalm-singing, hymns, prayer, and preaching, it was devising a new thing, and in its transformation of the medieval Mass, while it summoned the laity once again to a legitimate participation in the Church's central rite, it gave them a rite which was shorn of some of its essential elements and performed by ministers who lacked the apostolic commission which the Church had hitherto guarded by regular ordination. In the light of the worship of the early Church the recovery of the true position of the laity was therefore fictitious.

2. *The Clergy and their Assistants.* The rejection of the threefold ministry was less eager and less absolute among the Lutherans than among the followers of Zwingli and Calvin, but the underlying principle was the same and the issue was the same, except in Scandinavia. In Luther's opinion the sacrament of Orders was " nothing else than a cere-

mony for choosing preachers." The ministry itself was a divine institution, having as its function the preaching of the Gospel and the administration of the sacraments, but the forms of the ministry were not divinely appointed but left to the needs and discretion of the Church. Each German State was free to devise its own system of pastorates, and the prince became the organizer and the head. Pastors were free to marry ; and, though the familiar vestments were worn in some places as late as the eighteenth century, and have persisted down to our own time in the Lutheran Church in Scandinavia, the surplice or black gown and bands began to displace them in early days. In Calvin's system there was more precision, and the four orders of pastor, doctor, elder, and deacon, were instituted for the government of the Church.

3. *The Religious Orders*. It was no longer held that monks conferred any benefit upon the community at large, and the Religious Orders were therefore dissolved. Monks and nuns renounced their vows, returned to the world, and married ; and in view of the corruption of many of the monastic houses in Germany and the Netherlands this conclusion to a scandalous degeneracy may be held to be necessary and right. Yet there was no real compensation for the loss of that large element in the Church's worship which is contributed by the Religious Orders.

II.—PLACES OF WORSHIP; AND LITURGICAL BOOKS AND MUSIC

1. *Places of Worship.* Renaissance architecture, which was based upon the Doric, Ionic, and Corinthian orders of classical times, came to birth in Italy, where the Gothic style had never succeeded in establishing itself securely. It spread slowly from Italy to the other countries of western Europe, meeting there with a stronger opposition, and frequently being combined with Gothic elements. In some of the Renaissance churches of the fifteenth century there appeared for the first time a gradine, or shelf above the altar, used as a stand for the candlesticks. This novelty was destined to grow to such evil proportions in later days as to give the altar the appearance of a mere pediment for the support of the ornaments that were piled above it, frequently without regard to the reredos which they obscured. It was probably during the papal sojourn at Avignon that the practice was there introduced of increasing the number of lights set upon the altar by placing upon it the seven tapers carried in procession by acolytes. This use was subsequently adopted in other Continental churches, the middle taper being withdrawn except when a bishop was officiating.

Luther's treatment of church ornaments was very

different from that of Zwingli and Calvin. Wherea
the latter destroyed everything for which no explici
scriptural sanction was to be found, altars and thei
equipment, shrines and images, pictures, organs
and bells, all being broken up, the Lutherans tool
the line that things which the Bible did not forbic
might be permitted, and they retained even crucifixe:
and tabernacles, though they made no use of the
latter. As to the churches, there were varying
measures of interior adaptation according to need
but the buildings themselves were generally allowec
to stand unchanged, except in the case of monasterie:
and convents. The beginnings of Protestant architecture were hardly to be seen until a century hac
passed.

2. *Liturgical Books and Music.* At the beginning
of 1522 a document entitled *Ordnung der Stad.
Wittenberg* was issued in Luther's absence; and
later in the same year the first German Mass wa:
produced by Kantz, the Prior of the Carmelite
brothers at Nördlingen. In 1523 Müntzer followec
it with a notable attempt at a German liturgy and a
form of Daily Office.

Luther himself issued a series of theological and
liturgical treatises from 1523 onwards, the chief o:
which were *Taufbüchlein* (1523), a German translation of the Order of Baptism with very little change ;
Von Ordnung Gottesdiensts in der Gemeine (1523), an

ssay prescribing the Church's daily worship; *Formula Missae et Communionis pro ecclesia Vittem-ergensi* (1523), a detailed exposition and order of the Mass in Latin; and *Deutsche Messe und Ordnung Gottesdiensts* (1526), a German Mass and daily ser-vices. It was Luther's intention to legislate for Wittenberg alone, but after the visitation instituted by Duke John Frederick in 1527 his regulations were enforced throughout Saxony.

Visitations undertaken in their own territories by other princes resulted in the issue of a number of *Kirchenordnungen* (Church Orders), based in general upon Luther's work, but sometimes betraying a greater degree of conservatism. Examples of these Orders are that of Nuremberg (1525) and that of Riga (1530), the *Brandenburg-Nuremberg Order* (1533), the *Saxon Church Order* (1539), the *Brandenburg Order* 1540), the *Calenberg and Göttingen Order* (1542), the *Schleswig-Holstein Order* (1542), and the *Pfalz-Neuberg Order* (1543).

As a result of the desire of Hermann von Wied, Archbishop of Cologne, to reform his own diocese, an important document appeared in German in 1543, and in Latin in 1545 under the title *Simplex ac ia deliberatio*, which, though it proved abortive in Germany, was put to great use by Cranmer in his reform of the services of the English Church.

In Switzerland Zwingli issued in 1523 a conservative work entitled *De canone missae epicheiresis*, and in 1525 the revolutionary *Action oder Bruch des Nacht mals*; Oecolampadius issued his Basle liturgy in 1525; a French reformed liturgy, *La maniere e fasson*, believed to be the work of Farel, appeared in 1533; Calvin produced two doctrinal works, his great *Institutio Christianae Religionis* in 1536 and his *Petit Traicte de le Cene* in 1541; and in 1542 the standard Calvinistic liturgy appeared at Geneva under the title *La forme de prieres, etc.*

The fourteenth century carried on the great development of Church music which was centred in the Paris School of Perotin and his fellows and in the fifteenth and sixteenth centuries there was a rich development at the hands of Dufay Obrecht, Josquin des Prés, Orlando di Lasso and many another in the Netherlands, and of Festa, Palestrina, Allegri, and others in Italy, as well as in Spain and Germany. At the same time, a completely new turn in the Church's use of music was given by the Reformation. In Germany Martin Luther, following the example set by the leaders of the Bohemian Brethren, gave the people hymns in their own tongue and made hymn singing an important element in congregational worship; and in Switzerland Calvin similarly developed psalmody. Agreeing in their rejection of the words of the Latin hymns, so many of which had

reference to the Blessed Virgin Mary and the Mass,
they differed as to the most desirable substitute,
Luther rekindling the Old German vernacular song
and composing new hymns out of his own devotional experience, Calvin preferring to restrict himself to the use of the inspired poetry of the Psalter.
And as to tunes, while Calvin rejected the old and
replaced them with noble melodies collected and
composed by Bourgeois and others, Luther with
more catholic taste adapted some of the existing
music of the Church, borrowed from the chorales
which probably represent German folk-melodies,
and added to these treasures magnificent tunes
composed by himself and his friends, his chief
collaborator being Walther.

IV.—INITIATION AND ECCLESIASTICAL DISCIPLINE

1. *Initiation*. In Germany both Baptism and
Confirmation were retained, with modifications, the
former being administered normally to infants and
the latter to children after instruction. Luther's
Taufbüchlein, which appeared in 1523, was little more
than a German translation of the Latin Order of
Baptism; but in 1526, when Luther revised the
Order, he retained only one exorcism and he
omitted the ceremonies associated with the use of
salt, spittle, chrism, the white garment, and the
taper. Hermann's *Simplex ac pia deliberatio*, which

was mainly the work of Bucer so far as ritual is concerned, provided for the administration of Baptism in two parts on consecutive days. The first part included an exhortation to the sponsors, questions leading to renunciations and a confession of faith, signing with the cross, exorcism and prayer, the Gospel with an exposition, the Lord's Prayer and the Creed, a psalm and a Collect. The second part, the Baptism proper, took place on the following day in the course of the Mass. After the Creed an Epistle and Gospel were read, a prayer of intercession was made, Baptism was administered, and a prayer and a hymn followed. In the completion of Baptism by Confirmation the chief change resulted from the disappearance of the episcopate. The laying on of hands was administered by pastors, without the use of chrism, which was declared to be " superfluous," and without the sign of the cross. Its sacramental significance was further obscured by the stress laid upon the sufficiency of the candidate's knowledge and upon the public declaration of his intention to fulfil his baptismal vows.

Zwingli and Calvin both insisted upon Infant Baptism, the former regarding it frankly as an edifying ceremony of dedication and a sign of allegiance, the latter sharing the Church's faith in the imparting of spiritual benefit, but supposing it to be limited to the elect. Among the Calvinists Baptism was administered at Catechism-time on Sundays and at sermon-time on other days. After exhortation and prayer the sponsors were required to make the customary promises, and baptism by affusion followed, in the Name of the Trinity. Confirmation degenerated into a formal admission to the Lord's Supper, after a course of instruction.

The Anabaptists, or re-baptizers, who arose at Zürich and Wittenberg, and appear to have propagated their revolutionary doctrines far and wide, though they produced no outstanding leader, rejected Infant Baptism in favour of Believers' Baptism, which was administered to adolescents and adults, generally at first by the usual method of affusion, but sometimes by immersion, which later became their rule.

2. *Ecclesiastical Discipline.* Out of the many evils which exposed the Church of the Renaissance period to the criticism and attack of right-minded men, the sale of indulgences was seized upon by Luther and Zwingli independently as the most intolerable. With their vigorous rejection of this abuse the Reformers abandoned also the medieval conception of the working of the sacrament of penance ; but they recognized the necessity of preparation for Communion on the part of communicants, and of some means of testing fitness on the part of the authorities of the Church. Among the

Lutherans admission to Communion was conditioned by freedom from open and unrepented sin, and by success in a yearly examination on the nature and purpose of Communion, except in cases where this was held to be unnecessary. In addition to this, Luther strongly recommended the voluntary use of private confession ; but the practice gradually died out. Zwingli appointed a court of discipline for the purpose of excluding unworthy communicants ; and Calvin soon departed from his early recommendation of voluntary private confession and trusted to the vigilance of the Consistory, a body of six Pastors and twelve Elders, who met weekly to receive reports on the visitation of Genevan households.

V.—CORPORATE WORSHIP

1. *The Eucharist.* During the transitional period between the Middle Ages and the Reformation Age the Mass was regarded largely as a means of procuring relief for the souls in Purgatory ; and the many priests who were maintained by money bequeathed for the purchase of such relief were in duty bound to regard the offering of Masses for the dead as their first, and often as their only, duty. At the Parish Mass the Communion of the people was more infrequent than ever it had been before, a great proportion of the Faithful contenting them-

selves with an annual Communion at Easter. The withholding of the chalice from the laity had been for some time a growing practice ; and it was finally decreed by the Council of Constance (1414-1418) and by the Council of Basle (1431-1449) that the laity, and also the clergy when not celebrating, were not bound to communicate in both kinds. Thus the Reformers came to rule out the sacrificial significance of the Mass, which had been so greatly distorted ; they restored its fellowship-significance and increased the frequency of its use as a means of Communion ; and they returned to the divinely appointed rule of Communion in both kinds. In addition to these things, they substituted the language of the people for the Latin which was no longer understood ; though in Germany this substitution was carried out only gradually.

Luther appears to have desired to move slowly at first in the reform of the Mass ; and he reversed unauthorized changes made by Carlstadt in 1521 at the Christmas Communion at Wittenberg and more formally in the *Ordnung der Stadt Wittenberg* in January of the following year. He deplored admission to Communion without the preliminary confession ; he caused the Latin tongue to be used again in the Narrative of Institution ; and he restored the practice of elevation. In 1522, however, Prior Kantz drew up a German liturgy for the Carmelites at Nördlingen, which substituted an exhortation and introductory prayers for the *Missa catechumenorum*; in 1523 Thomas Müntzer issued a German Daily Office and Mass, providing in the latter for the use of variable forms at Advent, Christmas, Passiontide, Easter, and Pentecost; and in the same year Oecolampadius produced a third German rite in a work entitled *Das Testament Jesu Christi*, which appears to have been intended for devotional use. By this time Luther, who seems to have known no other liturgy than the Latin Mass, persuaded himself to undertake a conservative liturgical revision. In *Von Ordnung Gottesdiensts in der Gemeine* (1523) he ordered the cessation of the daily Mass and the association of Communion and a sermon with the Sunday Mass; and later in the year he issued a revised Latin rite entitled *Formula Missae et Communionis*. In this rite Luther allowed the part before the Canon to stand almost unchanged; but the Canon itself he revised drastically so as to purge it of its sacrificial intention, and for reasons which can only be surmised he made the Sanctus and Benedictus follow the Narrative of Institution. In 1526 appeared Luther's *Deutsche Messe*, which set the standard for all subsequent liturgies of the more liberal type in northern and central Germany, as did the *Formula* for the more conservative group; in 1533 there came the Brandenburg-Nuremberg rite,

which may be taken as representative of the results
of a process of disciplinary reduction of local variations to a common Lutheran standard; and in
1543-5 Hermann issued, in his *Simplex ac pia
deliberatio*, a rite which assisted to determine the
English reform of the liturgy. The structure of
these rites may be seen in the table on pages 148
and 149.

On a general view of the Lutheran reform of the
Mass the conservative element appears in the reten-
tion of the Eucharist as the chief act of Sunday
worship, in a certain unwillingness to dispense
completely with the use of Latin, in the general
continuance of the vestments, wafer bread, the sign
of the cross over the elements, the sacring bell, and
the act of kneeling to receive the sacred Gifts;
whereas the reforming element is seen in the omission of all sacrificial language in the rite and in the
rearrangement of its parts, in the insistence upon
the sermon and the abundant provision for the
singing of psalms and hymns, in the restoration of
the chalice to the laity, and in the common though
not invariable practice of administering the Bread
before the consecration of the chalice.

At Zürich, two years after the issue of Zwingli's
Epicheiresis, in which, like Luther, he retained most
of the first part of the Mass and rejected the Canon,
but, unlike Luther, provided prayers to take the

Medieval Mass	Deutsche Messe, 1526	Brandenburg-Nuremberg Rite, 1533	Hermann's Rite, 1543–5
I	I	I	I
			Confession and Absolution.
Introit.	Psalm or Hymn.	Introit or Hymn.	Introit (Latin).
Kyrie.	Kyrie.	Kyrie.	Kyrie.
Gloria in excelsis.		Gloria in excelsis.	Gloria in excelsis.
Collect.	Collect.	Collect.	Collect.
Epistle.	Epistle.	Epistle.	Epistle.
Gradual and Alleluia.	Hymn.	Alleluia or Gradual.	Alleluia or Gradual or Sequence, and Hymn.
Gospel.	Gospel.	Gospel.	Gospel.
(Sermon.)			Sermon.
			Prayer of Intercession.
Creed.	Creed (metrical).	Creed.	Creed and Offering.
	Sermon.	Sermon.	
II	II	II	II
Oremus.			
Offertory.			

148

Sursum corda. Preface. Sanctus. CANON. (*See p.* 86)	Paraphrase of Lord's Prayer. Exhortation to Communicants. Narrative of Institution.	Exhortation to Communicants. Narrative of Institution. Sanctus. Lord's Prayer.	Sursum corda. Preface (invariable). Sanctus. Narrative of Institution. Lord's Prayer.
Fraction and Communion. Agnus Dei. Pax.		" The peace of the Lord . . .,"	
Prayers. Communion, with *Communio.*	Communion, with Hymns, including versified *Sanctus* and *Agnus.*	Communion, *Agnus* or *Communio.*	Communion, with *Agnus* and Hymn.
	Thanksgiving.	Thanksgiving.	Thanksgiving.
Collect. Dismissal.	Benediction.	Benediction.	Benediction.

place of the Canon, Zwingli issued his *Action oder Bruch des Nachtmals*, which provided for the transformation of the Mass into a love-feast of remembrance, to be held at Easter, at Pentecost, once in the autumn, and at Christmas. Vestments, music, and singing were disallowed; the altar became a table, from which bread and wine were distributed to the seated congregation; and for the liturgy was substituted a sermon, a fixed epistle (1 Cor. xi. 20–29), the recitation of *Gloria in excelsis*, a fixed gospel (John vi. 47–63), the Apostles' Creed, an exhortation and a prayer, the reading of the Narrative of Institution, the distribution of the bread and wine, the recitation of Psalm cxiii. as a thanksgiving for the redemption thus commemorated, and the dismissal.

Calvin, who had sketched a form for the Lord's Supper in his *Institutio* in 1536, was expelled from Geneva in 1538 and, on taking charge of the French Reformed congregation at Strassburg, found there a much simplified revision of a conservative German Mass which had been introduced as far back as 1524. This rite was adopted and modified by Calvin. In 1541 he carried it with him on his return to Geneva, where a rite attributed to Farel and known as *La maniere et fasson* was then in use. In 1542 Calvin produced from the Strassburg rite and the Genevan rite an order entitled *La forme de prieres et chantz ecclesiastiques avec la maniere d'administrer les sacrements, etc.*, which includes the norm of Reformed Communion Services under the heading *La maniere de celebrer la cene.* In this rite prayer for the Church is followed by a long exhortation to communicants; the people then come up to the table to receive the bread and wine standing, psalms being sung meanwhile or suitable passages of Scripture read; and after a prayer of thanksgiving and the singing of Nunc Dimittis, the blessing is given.

2. *The Daily Office.* In Lutheran Germany the highly complicated medieval Daily Office was everywhere reduced, in varying resultant forms, to two daily services in the vernacular. Luther's order, set forth in 1526 in his *Deutsche Messe und Ordnung Gottesdiensts*, provided for a service at 5 or 6 a.m. on Sundays and festivals, consisting of psalms, a sermon on the Epistle, an anthem, Te Deum or Benedictus, the Lord's Prayer and a Collect. Mass followed at 8 or 9 a.m. And in the afternoon Vespers completed the day's services, with a sermon on the Old Testament after Magnificat. On weekdays a service similar to the Sunday morning service was provided in the early morning and late afternoon, but was intended mainly for school-children.

Zwingli substituted daily Bible-readings and preaching for the Mass and the Office; and on Sundays he provided services at 8 a.m. and 4 p.m.

with the added elements of psalms, prayers, and the Creed, while a special service for children and servants was held at midday. Calvin arranged for preaching in the early morning on Mondays, Wednesdays, and Fridays ; and on Sundays there was an early service which consisted of a confession, a psalm, extempore prayer, and a sermon, followed by intercessions, the Apostles' Creed, and the blessing. A catechism for children was held at midday ; and at 3 p.m. there was more preaching.

3. *Litanies and Processions*. These were abandoned in Switzerland ; but in Germany the use of the litany was retained. In 1529 Luther issued, first in Latin and then in German, a litany based upon the familiar medieval forms, but omitting the invocation of saints and supplying new petitions and Collects. Litanies were ordered by some of the *Kirchenordnungen* to be said on Wednesdays or Fridays, or on both days ; and Hermann suggested their use once a week in towns, on Wednesday or Friday, and once a month in villages.

4. *Preaching and Teaching*. Before the Reformation the preacher's task in the parish church was commonly confined to the exposition of the Gospel at Mass. These homilies were known as Postils, a word of uncertain origin ; and they were frequently drawn from one of the " Sleepwells " that were provided at this time for the use of preachers unequal

to their task.   The most famous of these compilations was entitled *Dormi secure* (Sleep without care),
which was the work of John of Werden (*d.* 1437),
a Franciscan of Cologne.   The clergy found this
book so valuable an aid to untroubled sleep on
Saturday nights that they consumed twenty-five
editions of it before the end of the fifteenth century.

Yet there were preachers of merit, and even some
of great excellence, in every country of Western
Europe during the pre-Reformation age ; and a few
among them displayed in their sermons a prophetic
zeal for the reform of morals and of ecclesiastical
abuses.   In Italy the learned Dominican, Leonardo
of Utino (*d.* 1470), the popular and dramatic
Franciscan, John of Capistrano (*d.* 1486), and the
gifted Franciscans, Bernardino of Busti and Robert
Caracciolo of Lecce, generally supported the existing order ; while the scholarly Franciscan, St.
Bernardino of Siena (*d.* 1444), the famous Dominican, Gabriel Barletta, and Savonarola (*d.* 1498), by
far the greatest of them all, strove for reform.   In
France the two most popular preachers were the
Franciscans, Oliver Maillard and Michel Menot,
both of whom satirized their age and lashed its
vices.   In the Netherlands reform was preached by
Gerhard Groot (*d.* 1384), the founder of the
Brethren of the Common Life.   In Germany John
Gritsch (*d.* 1430), Gabriel Biel (*d.* 1495), and John

Geiler of Kaisersburg (*d.* 1510), stood for the old order; while John Richsrath (*d.* 1481) was a vehement preacher of reform. In Bohemia the bold pioneer, Conrad of Waldhausen (*d.* 1369), the diligent and persistent John Milicz (*d.* 1374), and the great John Hus (*d.* 1415), were all on the side of reform.

When the storm of the Reformation burst upon Europe, it was inevitable that there should be much preaching and teaching for the commendation or the combating of the reformers' views, and it was inevitable also that a new reality and a new vigour should characterize the work of preaching. In the districts where the Reformation was accepted the Bible was put into the hands of the people and was read in the vernacular at all services; the preachers expounded it so as to discredit medieval errors and to establish from it the doctrines which they held to be of vital importance; and catechetical instructions for children and young people were drawn up and systematically taught. Of these catechisms Luther himself was responsible for a " Greater Catechism " and a " Short Catechism " in 1529; Calvin's *Instruction et Confession de Foi*, which appeared in 1537, gave place to the *Catechismus Genevensis*, which was published in French in 1541, and in Latin in 1545; and the famous *Heidelberg Catechism*, compiled by Ursinus and Olevianus, was published in 1563.

The outstanding preachers of reform in Germany were Martin Luther (1483–1546), virile and downright, master of the language of the people, and rich in sympathy ; Veit Dietrich (d. 1549), one of his younger friends, gifted with a power of simple utterance and a humble devotion ; Justus Jonas (d. 1555), Luther's trusted companion, learned and eloquent ; John Bugenhagen (d. 1558), pastor at Wittenberg, great alike as organizer and teacher ; Caspar Aquila (d. 1560), vivid and vehement ; John Brentz (d. 1570), an expository preacher of power ; and Wolfgang Capito (d. 1541) and Martin Bucer (d. 1551), who laboured together at Strassburg. In Switzerland the powerful Huldreich Zwingli (1484–1531), the Anabaptist, Balthasar Hübmaier (d. 1528), the scholarly Leo Jud (d. 1542), and the strenuous Henry Bullinger (d. 1575), who succeeded Zwingli as leader, were associated with Zürich ; John Oecolampadius (d. 1531) and Oswald Myconius (d. 1552) worked diligently at Basle ; Bern was the scene of the labours of Berthold Haller (d. 1536) ; and John Calvin (1509–1564), masterly expositor, splendidly lucid in thought and style, dominated Geneva. In France the greatest of the reforming preachers were the tempestuous and moving William Farel (d. 1565), the gentler Pierre Viret (d. 1571), and their colleague, Antoine Froment (d. 1581).

VI.—THE HALLOWING OF LIFE

1. *Festivals and Fasts.* Lutheranism retained the general framework of the Church's Year and continued to observe the more important festivals. Calvinism, on the contrary, kept only the Lord's Day, completely abandoning all other festivals on the twofold ground of lack of scriptural authority and of the danger of superstitious associations ; but it recognized the value of fasting as a disciplinary exercise, and its congregations were sometimes called to observe specially appointed days which had no relation to the fast-days of the medieval Church.

2. *Marriage.* Luther, in his *Traubüchlein* of 1534, and Hermann in his *Deliberatio* of 1543-5, provided marriage services in the vernacular ; and Calvin ordered that, after banns had been duly read, marriage might take place before the sermon on any day of the week. The service was completely dissociated from the Holy Communion.

3. *Sickness and Death.* Among the Lutherans importance was attached to the administration of the sacrament of Holy Communion to the sick ; and, though reservation for this purpose was not immediately abandoned, it gradually became the custom to consecrate in the sick man's room, friends being required to share the Communion with him. The burial of the dead was provided for

by a seemly Office, shorn of medieval ceremonies and purgatorial apprehension. Masses for the dead were abolished.

Calvinist practice varied considerably at first ; but, while the sick were visited and prayed for, the custom of administering Communion to them was gradually abandoned. And as to the dead, they were just buried, " without superstition," and no prayer was offered on their behalf.

VII.—POPULAR DEVOTIONS

Bible-reading, prayer-meetings, and the singing of psalms and hymns, supplanted the numerous forms of popular medieval devotion.

CHAPTER VI

THE REFORMATION IN GREAT BRITAIN AND IRELAND

I.—A SURVEY OF THE PERIOD

The Reformation of the Church of England, which covers the period from 1534 to 1662, resulted from the same causes as those which provoked the Continental Reformation, and was fully exposed to its influence. Its main resultant was, however, wholly different. Continental reform began with an attempt to remove medieval abuses; it went on to reject the unyielding authority of the Bishop of Rome; and it ended by creating new systems of doctrine and organization and practice which took to themselves the common title of Protestantism and were set in the field as rivals, not merely to papalism and the medieval corruption of Catholicism, but to Catholicism itself. In England, on the contrary, reform began with a royal repudiation of the authority of the Pope; it went on to the removal of medieval abuses and to the revision of liturgical forms, at one stage with a dangerous zeal and a Protestant temper, but never with the reckless abandonment of accustomed use which characterized the Continental Reformation; and it ended by presenting as its main result a reformed Catholicism which included all the essentials of continuity with the Apostolic Church but was not *Roman* Catholic, while it embraced certain principles which were held also by Protestants and yet had nothing in common with the novel and revolutionary spirit of the Protestant sects. Outside the reformed Church of England in which this non-papal Catholicism was expressed, there remained in this country some Catholics who continued their allegiance to the Pope and their loyalty to the medieval system in which they had been nurtured; and until the restoration of the monarchy in 1660 Protestantism maintained an unceasing struggle with Anglicanism from within and without the borders of the national Church. After that year its forces began to be concentrated in non-conforming sects outside the Church of England.

England's repudiation of the papal control of the ecclesiastical courts resulted from the desire of Henry VIII to obtain a divorce from Catharine of Aragon. The reformation which followed resulted from the abuses of the medieval Church and the sins of its rulers, and was linked on to the old rebellion of Wyclif and the Lollards. By 1534 the breach with Rome was complete; and, though Henry himself was opposed to any serious changes, the way was clear for effecting subsequently the many reforms which had been frequently demanded and as frequently refused. By 1539 all the monasteries had been dissolved and their wealth appropriated; shrines were despoiled and images forbidden; the Bible in English was ordered to be set up in the churches in 1538; and Cranmer's English Litany was issued in 1544. Otherwise the services continued to be read in Latin, a measure of uniformity being secured by the imposition of the secular Sarum Breviary on the whole Province of Canterbury by order of Convocation in 1542.

On the accession of the boy-king Edward VI in 1547, however, liturgical reform proceeded apace and became increasingly subject to Protestant influence. The First Prayer-Book, containing all the services, revised and in English, came from Cranmer's hands in 1549. It was supplemented by the Ordinal in the following year; and the whole was again revised and issued as the Second Prayer-Book in 1552. Mary succeeded to the throne in 1553, and called a halt. Submission was made to the Pope, the old service-books in Latin were taken into use again, and reformers were expelled or subjected to violent persecution. Elizabeth, who became queen in 1558 and reigned until 1603, once more asserted the Church's independence of the Pope, who excommunicated her in 1570; she provided for the restoration of the English Prayer-Book, slightly revised on lines which more effectually safeguarded the Church's Catholic position and yielded nothing to the Puritans ; and by arranging for the due consecration of Matthew Parker as Archbishop of Canterbury in 1559 she assisted in preserving the apostolic succession of the ministry at a time of grave crisis in the fortunes of the English Church.

In Scotland the work of reform which had been set on foot mainly by George Wishart in 1542 was vehemently carried forward by John Knox ; and in 1560 Catholicism was replaced by a system compounded of Calvinism and incipient Presbyterianism.   After the death of Knox in 1572 the process of reform continued, and issued in the establishment of thorough-going Presbyterianism, at the hands of Andrew Melville, in 1592.   In Ireland, apart from the imported Presbyterianism of the north, the Reformation produced but little effect, the great majority of the people remaining loyal to Rome.

The accession of James VI of Scotland to the English throne in 1603 raised hopes among the Presbyterians which were dashed to the ground at the Hampton Court Conference in 1604. The English Prayer-Book continued in use with some minor alterations ; the Authorized Version of the Bible was issued in 1611 ; and the able work of Archbishop Parker and Richard Hooker in expounding the true character of Anglicanism was carried on by a succession of notable divines, chief among whom was the saintly Bishop Lancelot Andrewes. Under Charles I Archbishop Laud continued the literary defence and exposition of Anglicanism and undertook the prosecution of an active policy which was intended to promote discipline and a moderate uniformity in the Church. This added fuel to the political troubles which were accumulating ; while in Scotland, where the episcopacy that was broken in 1560 had been restored in 1610, the introduction of a new Prayer-Book drawn up by some Scottish bishops in 1637 led to revolution in the following year and the re-establishment of Presbyterianism. When the Civil War began in 1642 and the Scots were brought in on the side of the king's enemies, the combined forces of Presbyterians, Anabaptists, and Independents turned the tide of Anglicanism and made strong headway against it. The Westminster Assembly of Divines, which sat from 1643 to 1648, issued *A Directory for the Public Worship of God throughout the Three Kingdoms*, which superseded the use of the Prayer-Book ; many of the clergy were ejected from their livings ; and the grievous work of puritanical destruction in the cathedral and parish churches was begun. Under Cromwell's rule Independency became the recognized religion of England, though toleration was shown to all other forms except Antinomianism, Anglicanism, and Roman Catholicism. The Society of Friends (Quakers) was formed at this time by George Fox.

At the Restoration the Church of England once more came into its own, and Scotland also witnessed the restoration of episcopacy. The Savoy Conference of 1661 resulted in the Church's final rejection of Puritan claims ; the Book of Common Prayer was thoroughly revised, attaining a form which was nearer to the standards of the First Prayer-Book than any of its predecessors ; and as a result of the Act of Uniformity in 1662 the Church lost large numbers of those who were not truly of its mind and spirit. For conscience' sake they went out into Non-conformity or Dissent.

II.—ESTATES OF MEN AND THEIR FUNCTIONS IN WORSHIP

1. *The Laity.* The medieval Church in England had its critics, its heretics, and its lax and defiant members to deal with ; but the great mass of the people believed in it, cared for their parish churches, and used them diligently according to the system in which they had grown up. The reformation of the Church inevitably promoted controversy, disaffection, and disobedience, among both liberals and conservatives ; and the attempt made, by means of

a series of Acts of Uniformity, to retain the whole population of the land within the borders of the national Church proved a failure. The transition from a corrupt but long-established and authoritative system shared with all other lands in Western Europe, to a truer but unaccustomed and detached ecclesiastical organization and worship, effected the ultimate separation of the laity into a small body of adherents to the old order, a larger mixed body of Protestants, with ideals akin to those of the Continental reformers, and a majority who accepted the reforms carried out by the combined authority of Church and State and continued to use their parish churches, with a new sense of the meaning of common prayer.

2. *The Clergy and their Assistants.* Whereas the threefold ministry of bishops, priests, and deacons was almost everywhere abandoned by the reformers on the Continent, it was carefully retained in England in unbroken succession from the past; and by the rejection of papalism the bishops were given their proper status in the Church. The diaconate was unfortunately not restored to the dignity of a permanent type of ministry, as it had originally existed throughout the Church and still exists in the the East, but was continued merely as a convenient probation for the priesthood. The minor orders were rejected, as having no actual ministerial value;

and the clergy were brought into closer touch with the laity by being freed from the obligation to celibacy.

The English Ordinal, which first appeared in 1550, omitted the *traditio instrumentorum*, substituting for it the tradition of the Scriptures; it corrected the suggestion of the almost exclusive occupation of the priesthood with the sacrifice of the Mass, restoring a proper emphasis upon its pastoral and prophetic functions ; and it gave prominence to the imposition of hands and prayer to the Holy Spirit as the essential elements of ordination. The customary vestments of the clergy when ministering in the congregation were retained by the First Prayer-Book, almost completely rejected by the Second Prayer-Book, and restored again by the Third Prayer-Book in 1559, which required the use of the ornaments worn in the second year of the reign of Edward VI. This order was confirmed in 1662, though as a result of Puritan influence it was mainly ignored in practice.

English Papists were secretly ministered to at this time by missionary priests trained in seminaries abroad, Jesuits and others, at considerable risk to their persons ; while the Protestants broke with the past and devised for themselves new forms of ministry after the manner of the Continental Protestants.

3. *The Religious Orders.* The monasteries were shamefully despoiled and ruthlessly suppressed, good and bad alike suffering the same fate. As in

the Reformation countries on the Continent, so in England, there was a great gap left in the worship of the Church after a thousand years of daily sacrifice and praise.

III.—PLACES OF WORSHIP ; AND LITURGICAL BOOKS AND MUSIC

1. *Places of Worship.* When church building was resumed after the long interruption caused by the Black Death, the Gothic style of architecture stiffened into the form known as Perpendicular, a form peculiar to England, which persisted until church building was again checked by the Reformation. During that time, from the last quarter of the fourteenth century to the middle of the sixteenth century, many great and splendid parish churches were built and many existing churches were enlarged and modified, so that the Perpendicular style, with its emphasis on vertical lines, became predominant in most parts of the country. Noble towers and porches were reared ; a notable advance in the art of making stained glass was met by the provision of large windows ; masons and wood-carvers found full scope for their energies in the splendid elaboration of screens and canopies, fonts and pulpits, stalls and benches, and much panelling ; complicated vaulted roofs were built, frequently of an exquisite beauty ; and, in order to meet the

need created by the increased importance attached to Masses for the dead, numerous altars were founded in the larger churches, and chantry chapels were set up about them, where chantry priests performed the ministry for which the foundations had been created by benefactors.

The Reformation period seriously checked the work of building churches and witnessed a transition from the Gothic style to the Renaissance, which was generally adopted when church building revived again after the Restoration. The Tudor reformers robbed the churches of relics, images, roods, rood-lofts, and altars, but otherwise they left them to a large extent untouched, though frequently uncared for. In the first half of the seventeenth century there was a recovery of seemliness ; altars which had been moved into the chancel or body of the church were restored to the east end ; and worthy gifts were placed in many of the churches. But during the Commonwealth period the Puritans wantonly destroyed stained-glass windows, carved and sculptured work, altars and other ornaments, and wrought grievous damage to the churches generally.

2. *Liturgical Books and Music.*   In the later Middle Ages in England the *Consuetudinarium* and the *Ordinale*, the two books used by the clergy as guides to the correct performance of the Mass and the Daily Office through the complicated course of the

Church's Year, came to be known respectively as the *Customary* and the *Directory* or *Pie* (*Pye*) or *Pica*. In spite of the valuable help afforded by Clement Maydeston's *Directorium Sacerdotum*, which was printed by Caxton in 1487, " the number and hardness of the rules called the Pie " taxed the powers of the clergy unnecessarily and wasted much of their time. Simplification was therefore the keynote of the changes introduced at the Reformation, when it was decided that " all the whole realm shall have but one use," and the services were translated into English, abbreviated, and collected into one book.

The issue of Archbishop Cranmer's English *Litany* in 1544 and of his *Order of the Communion* in 1548 heralded the publication of the first *Book of Common Prayer* in 1549, which was ordered to be used throughout the Church of England from Whitsunday. This book, which drew slightly from Greek and Mozarabic sources, more largely from Lutheran sources, but most of all from the books of the Sarum Use, was at once subjected to severe criticism by both English and Continental Protestants. Having been revised so as to meet many of the criticisms offered, it appeared as the second Book of Common Prayer in 1552, and was suppressed by Queen Mary after having been in use for only a few months. In 1559 the book was restored, after a slight but significant revision in a more conservative spirit; and from time to time, during the reign of Elizabeth, supplementary prayers were issued. The accession of James I led to the publication of the fourth Book of Common Prayer in 1604, which remained in use until it was forbidden by Parliament in 1645 and superseded by the rules contained in a Protestant work known as *A Directory for the Public Worship of God throughout the Three Kingdoms.* When the monarchy was restored in 1660 the Book of Common Prayer was once more put into the hands of revisers, the most notable of whom were Cosin, Bishop of Durham, Sanderson, Bishop of Lincoln, and Wren, Bishop of Ely; and, having been issued in its fifth form in 1662, it remained unaltered until the present century.

In Scotland the Book of Common Prayer had to give place to a book produced by Knox, which was entitled *The Book of our Common Order.* This was authorized by the General Assembly in 1562 and enforced in 1564. In 1575 its title was changed to *The Psalms of David in English metre, with the Form of Prayers and Ministration of the Sacrament used in the Church of Scotland.* This book survived the restoration of episcopacy in 1610 and a series of attempts, notably that made in 1637, to introduce a service-book akin to the English Book of Common Prayer; but it was superseded in 1645 by the Directory of Public Worship mentioned above.

The music of the English Church just before the
Reformation began was greatly enriched by the
work of such men as Dunstable, Tallis, Tye, Fairfax,
Taverner, Shepherd, and Whyte. Speedy provision for the unisonal rendering of the English
service of Mattins and Evensong and the Holy
Communion, as presented in the Book of Common
Prayer of 1549, was made by John Merbecke, who
issued in 1550 *The Book of Common Praier Noted.*
The music of this book, which represented an
adaptation of the familiar plainsong and was printed
on a four-lined stave, continued in use until the
period of the Commonwealth, but had no very
great effect until it was rediscovered in the nineteenth century. The cathedrals maintained the
old tradition, enriched increasingly as time went
on; and for parish churches and colleges there
was issued in 1560 John Daye's collection of choral
music entitled *Certaine Notes, set forth in foure and three
partes, to be sung at Morning, Communion and Evening
Praier,* and in 1561 Barnard's *Collection of Church
Music.* These books included compositions by
Tallis, Taverner, Shepherd, Causton, Farrant, and
many others. Organs were used as before, until
the Puritans destroyed them in the early days of
the Commonwealth; and additional instruments
were occasionally employed.

Metrical psalmody provided the popular element

in the music of the Reformation in England and Scotland as in the non-Lutheran parts of the Continental Reform. The first provision for this was made by Sternhold, whose *Certayne Psalmes* (nineteen in number) appeared in 1548, these being increased to thirty-seven in the following year. Hopkins then added to them; and " Sternhold and Hopkins," or " The Old Version " as it was called, reached its definitive edition in 1562, and held the field until 1696, when " The New Version " of Tate and Brady appeared. In Scotland " Sternhold and Hopkins " was supplemented by Genevan and Scottish writers and remained in use until 1650, when it was displaced by a new version based upon that of Francis Rous, Provost of Eton, the number of the old tunes to which the psalms had been sung being greatly reduced.

In spite of an attempt by Miles Coverdale in 1539 to introduce Lutheran hymns into English worship by means of his *Goostly Psalmes and Spiritualle Songs*, and a further effort on the part of George Withers, who produced his *Hymns and Songs of the Church* in 1623, the reformed English Church made no use of hymn-singing for some two hundred years; but anthems written by such masters as Byrd and Gibbons and the composers named above were regularly sung in cathedral and other churches equipped with adequate choirs.

IV.—INITIATION AND ECCLESIASTICAL DISCIPLINE

1. *Initiation.* The twofold rite of initiation was maintained in the reformed English Church, unchanged in essentials, but delivered from the excessive ceremonial of the Middle Ages and marked by a tendency to increase the period of time intervening between the administration of its two parts, in consequence of a new stress upon the need of an understanding co-operation in catechumens at the final stage of their admission. The Anabaptists refused to administer Baptism until years of discretion had been attained; the Presbyterians and other Protestant groups continued to use Infant Baptism; but all alike dispensed with Bishoping, or Confirmation.

In the Book of Common Prayer the forms prescribed for Baptism and Confirmation appeared from the first as separate services. An alternative form for private Baptism was provided from 1549, and a form for adult Baptism was added in 1662. The Catechism, which prefaced the Order of Confirmation in the First Prayer-Book, remained in that position until 1662, when it was given an independent place between the Orders of Baptism and the Order of Confirmation. The concluding section on the sacraments was added in 1604.

The Baptismal Office of 1549, which was much indebted to Lutheran forms, required that the font should always hold water in readiness for baptisms, the water being changed at intervals of not more than one month and blessed according to a prescribed form which included the use of the sign of the cross. Children were to be brought to church by their godparents on the Sunday or Holyday following their birth, and to be baptized immediately before the second canticle at Mattins or Evensong. In the first part of the service, which took place at the church door, the child was named, signed on forehead and breast, and exorcised; the Gospel was read, and followed by a short exhortation; and, when the godparents had recited the Lord's Prayer and the Apostles' Creed, the priest added a prayer and led the company to the font, holding the child's right hand. After the renunciation of evil, the acceptance of the Faith, and the expression of desire for Baptism, all of which were made by the sponsors, the priest dipped the child into the water three times—on its right side, on its left side, and face downwards—pronouncing meanwhile the baptismal formula. It was directed that in the case of a weak child it would suffice to pour water upon it. The priest then put the white vesture, known as the chrisom, upon the child, and anointed its head; and the service concluded with an exhortation to the godparents.

Confirmation was administered by the bishop to

children who were approved and presented by their parish priest after being instructed in the Catechism. The Order given in the 1549 Prayer-Book omitted unction, but required the bishop to pray for the gifts of the Holy Spirit and to sign the candidates on the forehead and lay his hand on the head of each.

In the 1552 Prayer-Book it was provided that the whole of the baptismal service should take place at the font. The benediction of the font was included, in an indirect form, in the service itself; the exorcism of the child was omitted, as was also the giving of the chrisom; the threefold immersion was no longer required, but might be reduced to a single dipping; and the use of the sign of the cross was transferred from the introductory part of the service to the act of baptism. The Order of Confirmation omitted the use of the sign of the cross and the accompanying words spoken by the bishop.

The 1662 Prayer-Book restored the direct form of the benediction of the font, in the course of the baptismal service, and insisted upon the signing of the child; while it embodied in the Order of Confirmation a paragraph which had previously appeared as an introductory rubric, and required of candidates a formal renewal of their baptismal vows.

2. *Ecclesiastical Discipline*.   In order to retain the whole of the people within the English Church and to secure uniformity of worship and teaching within

that Church, two Acts of Uniformity were passed in the reign of Edward VI (in 1549 and 1552), three in the reign of Elizabeth (in 1559, 1571, and 1581), and one in the reign of Charles II (in 1662). The penalties attached to these various acts failed to effect their purpose; and in the end both the Recusants (Roman Catholics) and the Nonconformists had to be tolerated. Within the Church the Acts assisted to promote " one use," but conflicting views as to the nature of that use resulted in the persistence of a considerable diversity of practice. Canons, Articles, and Rubrics were liable to various interpretations, and, if custom so ordained, could be ignored without penalty.

Ecclesiastical discipline, in the stricter sense of the term, included the requirement that would-be communicants should be confirmed as well as baptized; it provided for the possibility of suspension from Communion, and even of excommunication; and it recognized the voluntary use of penance, throwing the responsibility upon the conscience of the sinner. General confessions were included in the Holy Communion from 1549, and in Morning and Evening Prayer from 1552; but particular confession was suggested and provided for in the Order for the Visitation of the Sick and in the exhortation in the Holy Communion; and, though its practice greatly dwindled, it seems never to have been lost.

A new service, entitled *A Commination* in 1552, was introduced into the Prayer-Book of 1549 for use on Ash Wednesday, presumably in place of the sentences of the Greater Excommunication which the medieval Church was accustomed to read at the beginning of Advent and Lent and on the Sundays after Whitsunday and the Feast of the Assumption. It seems to have been intended as a temporary substitute for that restoration of the " godly discipline " of the primitive Church which was declared to be " much to be wished."

V.—CORPORATE WORSHIP

1. *The Eucharist.* It was the chief aim of the reformers to remove the corruptions of the medieval Mass and to transform it into the Eucharist and Communion of the Church's early days. The revolutionary work of the Continental reformers gravely embarrassed the leaders of the English Church, and to a large extent spoiled their first and best attempt ; but, even so, the result embodied three important changes, and the makers of the Prayer-Book must be allowed to have achieved their aim, with the accompaniment of some regrettable losses and distortions. First, they made it clear that the Christian sacrifice consists not in the external presentation by the priest of transubstantiated Bread and Wine, but in the worshipful pleading, by him for all, of Christ's

" one, perfect, and all-sufficient sacrifice " and in the self-donation of the worshippers in union with Him and under cover of the prevailing sacrifice made by Him on their behalf. Second, they restored the note of thanksgiving to its proper strength. And third, they gave the act of Communion its right importance, and in obedience to the command of Christ they insisted upon the delivery of the chalice to all communicants.

The stages by which the Mass was transformed were as follows. In 1548 Cranmer issued an English *Order of Communion* to be used as a preparation for the Communion of the people, and to be inserted in the Latin Mass after the point at which the priest communicated. This included two Exhortations, the Invitation, Confession and Absolution, the Comfortable Words, the Prayer of Humble Access, the Words of Administration, and the Peace of God. When the First Book of Common Prayer appeared in 1549 all this was found in the English Liturgy, which otherwise kept close to the Church's customary developed plan, presenting as its only real novelty an Epiclesis which preceded the Narrative of Institution. In the Second Prayer-Book, of 1552, Protestant influence availed to shatter this " very godly order," as it was even then described, limiting the vision and the prayers of the Church to this present world, dislocating the Canon in grievous fashion, supplying new words of administration, and adding an unauthorized Black Rubric which denied the real Presence of our Lord. In 1559 the words of administration were prefaced by the words of the 1549 Book, the eucharistic vestments were restored, and the offending Black Rubric was omitted. In 1662 various new rubrical directions assisted to recover laudable ceremonies on the part of priest and people, significant changes of words were made in several places, and the Black Rubric was restored after it had been rendered entirely innocuous by a change of wording ; but the 1552 framework remained with all its faults, and continued to provoke the criticism of those Churchmen who recognized the superiority of the 1549 Order. The differences will be readily seen in the tables on pages 179–181.

Among those who regarded the English Liturgy as standing too near to the Mass which they abhorred, it was the custom, in both England and Scotland, to fashion the celebration of the Lord's Supper on Calvinist and Zwinglian models ; and the Scottish Presbyterians offered a successful resistance to the use of what is incorrectly known as " Laud's Liturgy " of 1637, a notable Order which approximated closely to that of the 1549 Book of Common Prayer and was subsequently adapted by the Nonjurors for their use.

SARUM	1549	1552–1662
Preparation.	Lord's Prayer and Collect for Purity.	Lord's Prayer and Collect for Purity.
Introit.	Introit.	Decalogue and Kyries.
Kyrie.	Kyrie.	
Gloria in excelsis.	Gloria in excelsis.	
Collect.	Collect.	Collect.
	Prayer for the King.	Prayer for the King. (To precede Collect in 1662.)
Epistle.	Epistle.	Epistle.
Gradual.		
Gospel.	Gospel.	Gospel.
Creed.	Creed (and Sermon).	Creed (and Sermon).
Salutation, Response, and Bidding.	Exhortation.	
Offertory and Prayer.	Offertory and Sentence.	Offertory and Sentence.
		Prayer for the Church Militant.
		Exhortation.
		Invitation, Confession and Absolution, Comfortable Words.

SARUM	1549	1552–1662
Salutation, Sursum corda, and Preface.	Salutation, Sursum corda, and Preface.	Sursum corda and Preface.
Sanctus and Benedictus.	Sanctus and Benedictus.	Sanctus. Prayer of Humble Access.
CANON Prayer of oblation for the Church.	Prayer for the whole Church (the Living, the Saints, the Dead).	
Commemoration of the Living. Commemoration of the Saints.		
Prayer of oblation. Prayer for consecration.	Epiclesis.	Memorial of Redemption. Prayer for the Sacramental Gift.
Narrative of Institution.	Narrative of Institution. (Elevation forbidden.)	Narrative of Institution.
Anamnesis and Oblation. Commemoration of the Dead.	Anamnesis and Oblation.	

Prayer for the Living, and Commemoration of Saints.		
Conclusion, Consignation, and Elevation.		
Lord's Prayer.	Lord's Prayer.	
Fraction, Consignation, and Commixture.		
Agnus Dei.		
Pax.	Pax.	
	Invitation, Confession, and Absolution, Comfortable Words, Prayer of Humble Access.	
Communion.	Communion (Agnus Dei).	Communion.
Thanksgiving and Ablutions.		Lord's Prayer.
Post-Communion Prayer.	Post-Communion Sentence.	Prayer of Oblation or of Thanksgiving.
	Salutation, Response, and Prayer of Thanksgiving.	Gloria in excelsis.
Dismissal with Blessing.	Blessing.	Blessing.

2. *The Daily Office*.   In the Anglican revision of the Daily Office four changes of great importance were made.   First, the vulgar tongue alone was to be used, in order that the laity might be able to share in the performance of the daily *officium*. Second, it was arranged that consecutive sections of the psalter should be recited in regular course without the frequent interruptions and omissions caused by the observance of a greatly developed calendar.   Third, the Scripture lections were to be lengthened and so arranged that the greater part of the Bible was read in the course of a year.   And fourth, the common practice among the parochial clergy of reciting the eight parts of the Daily Office in two sections was adopted by the removal of medieval accretions and substitutes and by the compression of the Office proper into a morning and an evening service daily.

The use of the vernacular was already familiar in connexion with the Prymer, which contained certain of the psalms (and sometimes Collects, Epistles, and Gospels), and with the Bible.   In 1538 the English Bible was ordered to be set up in every church ; and in 1543 it was provided that a chapter of the New Testament should be read in English after *Te Deum* and *Magnificat* every Sunday and Holyday, the Old Testament being similarly used when the New Testament had been completed.   In

1544 Cranmer's English Litany appeared. Compline was sung in English in the King's Chapel in 1547; the Epistle and Gospel were ordered to be sung in English at High Mass in the same year; and the Mass itself was sometimes sung in English in 1548. In 1548 the English Order of the Communion was inserted in the Latin Mass; and with the appearance of the Book of Common Prayer in 1549 the sole use of the English tongue in the worship of the English Church was enforced. The admirable quality of Prayer-Book prose, the credit for which is due in large measure to Cranmer, gives the book a high place among the literary classics of the English people.

Since the ninth century the Gallican version of the psalter had been used in England, as elsewhere except in Rome. The translation prescribed for use in the English Daily Office appeared first in Coverdale's Bible of 1535, and was made from the "Douche (German) and Latyn." It was included in Matthew's Bible in 1537, and in the revision of that Bible made by Coverdale in 1539, known as the Great Bible; and it appeared in a revised form in a second edition in 1540. Through the adoption of the arrangement of the Hebrew psalter the enumeration of the English version differed from the Latin, which joined together Psalms ix. and x., and Psalms cxiv. and cxv., and divided Psalms cxvi. and cxlvii.

each into two parts. The 150 psalms were divided up into 60 groups, two of which were to be recited daily from the first day of the month to the thirtieth, the last two being repeated on the thirty-first day. Until 1662 special provision was made for February, the first two groups being recited on January 31 and the last two on March 1. Proper psalms were appointed only for Christmas Day, Easter Day, Ascension Day, and Whitsunday, from 1549 to 1662. In the latter year psalms were appointed also for Ash Wednesday and Good Friday.

The 1549 Lectionary took account of the ecclesiastical year only to the extent of providing Proper Lessons for some of the greater Holydays and of retaining the long-established custom of reading Isaiah during the season of Advent. For the rest it arranged that a chapter from the Old Testament and a chapter from the New Testament, neither more nor less, should be read morning and evening daily, Sundays and weekdays alike, from January 1 to December 31. The Books of Chronicles, the Song of Solomon, and parts of Ezekiel were omitted from the Old Testament; the Revelation was omitted from the New Testament; so that, with these exceptions, the Old Testament was read through, together with much of the Apocrypha, once in the course of each year, and the New Testament was read through three times in the year,

the Gospels and Acts in the morning and the
Epistles in the evening. In 1559 Proper Lessons
were prescribed from the Old Testament for every
Sunday in the year ; but otherwise no important
change was made in this very mechanical lectionary
until 1871.

Cranmer's work in compressing the Daily Office
into two parts seems to have advanced through four
stages. Making use at first of Cardinal Quignon's
revised Latin Breviary, he drew up a preliminary
scheme which retained the Latin tongue and the
customary Hours ; later he made a second draft
which used the vernacular for the Lord's Prayer and
the Lessons, and, by omitting Terce, Sext, None,
and Compline, and combining Mattins, Lauds, and
Prime, reduced the Hours to two ; his third
attempt, which owed much to Lutheran influence,
appeared in the Prayer-Book of 1549 ; and his
fourth was the revision of 1552. Abandoning
Terce, Sext, and None in his third scheme, Cranmer
drew from the Sarum Mattins, Lauds, and Prime
for his morning service, and from the Sarum
Vespers and Compline for his evening service.
To this result he added new introductory matter
in 1552, as may be seen in the table on pages
186 and 187.

The practice of including the eucharistic Collect
of the Day in the Daily Office, a practice which

SARUM SOURCE	1549	1552
	MORNING	PRAYER
		Sentence and Exhortation.
		Confession and Absolution.
Mattins	Lord's Prayer.	Lord's Prayer.
Mattins	Versicles and Gloria.	Versicles and Gloria.
Mattins	Venite and Psalms.	Venite and Psalms.
Mattins	Old Testament Lesson.	Old Testament Lesson.
Mattins	Te Deum or Benedicite.	Te Deum or Benedicite.
Lauds	New Testament Lesson.	New Testament Lesson.
Lauds	Benedictus.	Benedictus or Psalm c.
Prime	Kyrie.	Creed and Salutation.
Prime	Creed.	Kyrie.
Prime	Lord's Prayer.	Lord's Prayer.
Lauds	Preces.	Preces.
Lauds	Collect of the Day.	Collect of the Day.
Lauds	Collect for Peace.	Collect for Peace.
Prime	Collect for Grace.	Collect for Grace.
	EVENING	PRAYER
		Sentence and Exhortation.
		Confession and Absolution.
Vespers	Lord's Prayer.	Lord's Prayer.
Vespers	Versicles and Gloria.	Versicles and Gloria.
Vespers	Psalms.	Psalms.
Vespers	Old Testament Lesson.	Old Testament Lesson.
Vespers	Magnificat.	Magnificat or Psalm xcviii.
Compline	New Testament Lesson.	New Testament Lesson.
Compline	Nunc Dimittis.	Nunc Dimittis or Psalm lxvii.

SARUM SOURCE	1549	1552
	EVENING	PRAYER (*continued*)
Vespers	Kyrie.	Creed and Salutation.
Vespers	Creed.	Kyrie.
Vespers	Lord's Prayer.	Lord's Prayer.
Vespers	Preces.	Preces.
Vespers	Collect of the Day.	Collect of the Day.
Vespers	Collect for Peace.	Collect for Peace.
Compline	Collect for Aid.	Collect for Aid.

appears to have arisen in the eighth century, was continued by Cranmer, who showed remarkable skill both in translating the Latin Collects of the Sarum Missal and in composing new prayers on the same model. His work preserved for the use of the English Church ancient prayers and parts of prayers, many of which can be traced back to the Gregorian Sacramentary of the eighth century, some to the Gelasian Sacramentary of the seventh century, and a few even to the Leonine Sacramentary of the sixth century. Collects old and new were inserted also in other places in the Prayer-Book; various changes, substitutions, and additions were made in these and in the Proper Collects in the subsequent revisions of the Book, especially in 1662; and the term *Collect* came to be applied to more extended prayers lacking the formal structure and conciseness which characterize the Collect. As a general summary of the result, it may be said that, out of a total of some 200 prayers contained in the Prayer-Book of 1662, about one-half are in the true Collect form, and that nearly three-fourths of these can be traced, in whole or in part, to ancient sources.

In the 1549 Book it was ordered that the Athanasian Creed, so-called, should be sung or said after Benedicite on six specified feasts; and in 1552 the number of these was increased to thirteen. The singing of an anthem before or after the Office was permitted by the Elizabethan Injunctions of 1559; and a rubric authorizing this practice after the Third Collect was inserted in 1662.

In Scotland the Reformers dispensed with the Daily Office; but *The Book of our Common Order* provided for a morning service every Sunday which consisted of two parts. The reader's service included fixed prayers, the singing of psalms, and the reading of the Scriptures. The minister's service which followed included a psalm, a call to worship, free prayer, the sermon, prayer, the Creed, a psalm, and a blessing. Under the influence of the English Protestants this was reduced to a single service conducted by the minister, from which, strangely enough, the reading of the Bible was commonly omitted.

3. *Litanies and Processions : Miscellaneous Prayers.* In consequence of troubles caused by an excessive

rainfall in 1543 and war with Scotland and France in 1544, Cranmer prepared a new litany in the latter year; and for the encouragement of those who had " used to come slackly to the procession " he wrote it in English. Drawing his material mainly from three Sarum litanies, For Rogation Monday, For the Dying, and In Time of Trouble, and making use of a Lutheran litany of 1529 and of an Eastern litany taken from the Liturgy of St. Chrysostom, he produced a work of great excellence, which was included in Henry VIII's Prymer of 1545 and taken into use in that year. An Injunction of Edward VI, in 1547, forbad the singing of litanies in procession, and required the clergy to say or sing Cranmer's Litany immediately before High Mass, kneeling in the midst of the church. Processions did not cease, however, and they were expressly authorized in connexion with the observance of Rogationtide. In 1549 the Litany, deprived of three invocations of saints and angels which were originally included in it, appeared after the Holy Communion in the Book of Common Prayer and was ordered to be used before Mass on Wednesdays and Fridays, its continued use on Sundays probably being assumed. Gradually it attached itself, in practice, to Morning Prayer which preceded it; and in the 1662 Book it was ordered to be sung or said after Morning Prayer on Sundays, Wednesdays, and Fridays.

Its structure is that of a general litany followed by a Supplication for use in time of trouble. The general litany consists of four Invocations, six Deprecations, three Obsecrations, nineteen Intercessions, and two concluding Supplications, to which are added two Invocations, the Kyrie and the Lord's Prayer. The Supplication which follows is made up of a Versicle and Response, a Prayer, a Psalm-verse with Antiphon and Gloria, Versicles and Responses, two Prayers, and the Blessing.

Two prayers, for Rain and for Fair Weather, which were printed at the end of The Holy Communion in 1549, were transferred to the end of the Litany in 1552 and supplemented by three others; a Gregorian collect was added to these in 1559; and five prayers of thanksgiving were added in 1604. In 1662 all these prayers were gathered into a separate section, printed after the Litany, and headed *Prayers and Thanksgivings upon Several Occasions*; and they were increased by the addition of four intercessions and two thanksgivings. They were to be used, as desired, before the last two prayers of the Litany or of Morning and Evening Prayer, which received at this time the addition of five fixed prayers after the Third Collect. A separate section of supplementary *Forms of Prayer to be Used at Sea* was added to the Prayer-Book in 1662.

From the ninth century it had been the custom for

the priest to conduct from the pulpit after the sermon at Mass a brief vernacular service, known as
Prone, which included prayer, instruction, and the
giving of notices. This " bidding the bedes," or
praying the prayers, came to mean merely making
request for the prayers of the people, and was provided for by a Bidding Prayer prescribed by the
Elizabethan Injunctions of 1559 and by the fifty-fifth
of the Canons of 1604.

4. *Preaching and Teaching.* The stirring note of
reform which was heard in the preaching of John
Wyclif and his " poor priests " in the second half of
the fourteenth century died down in the century
which followed, but was not altogether silenced.
Though the Lollards, who maintained the protest,
produced no preachers of special renown, their insistence upon the use of the Bible and their vigorous
attacks upon the corruptions which marred the
Church's work commended themselves to the con-
sciences of many and helped to prepare the way for
the English Reformation of the sixteenth century in
general and for a greater estimation and use of
preaching in particular. John Colet, Dean of St.
Paul's, who died in 1519, two years after the beginning of the German Reformation, attracted many
Lollards to his congregations by his illuminating
expository preaching and his fearless denunciation
alike of images and of written sermons. Preaching

began to take on a fresh vigour; and there was a general abandonment of the formalism of the scholastic method, with its love of logical analysis and its use of numerous subdivisions, in favour of a more practical directness and simplicity.

In order to check the many novelties that inevitably appeared in the preaching of this period of critical debate and growing confusion, as a result of the free use of the Scriptures, there was issued in 1537 a book entitled *The Institution of a Christian Man*, but popularly known as *The Bishops' Book*, extracts from which were to be read to the people on Sundays and Holydays for three years. In 1543 a thoroughly revised and greatly improved edition of this work appeared under the title of *A Necessary Doctrine and Erudition for any Christian Man*, for which the name of *The King's Book* was substituted in popular usage. As a further protection against " rash preaching," and as a help to those who had no gift for preaching, Twelve Homilies were issued in 1547, the work of Cranmer and others; but even so there must have been many parishes where sound teaching of any description was wanting, for the visitations of the bishops at this time disclosed a woeful amount of ignorance and even illiteracy among the clergy. Two years later the First Prayer-Book required a sermon or homily in the traditional place, after the Creed at The Holy

Communion, but nowhere else ; and this requirement remained unchanged in all its subsequent
revisions.

The most notable of the preachers at this time
were Hugh Latimer, Bishop of Worcester, a man of
homely and witty speech and courageous vigour ;
Nicholas Ridley, Bishop of Rochester and afterwards
of London, a leading reformer and a scholar ; John
Hooper, Bishop of Gloucester, an outstanding
spokesman of the growing Puritanism ; and John
Bradford, scholarly, pious, and eloquent.   All these
met their death in 1555, when reform preaching was
being ruthlessly repressed by Queen Mary.

In pursuit of her policy of compromise and peace
Elizabeth forbad all contentious preaching at the
beginning of her reign ; and to the same end a
Second Book of Homilies, which was prepared in
1563, was authorized and taken into use in 1571.
This contained twenty-one sermons by various con-
tributors, of whom John Jewel, Bishop of Salisbury,
was the chief.   This scholarly prelate, who died in
1571, was one of the best of a number of men who
began at this time to give much care to the preparation of their sermons and to preach wisely and well
from their manuscripts in defence of true religion.
Greater even than Jewel was Richard Hooker (*d.*
1600), who wrote and preached with a rare dignity
and beauty of style for the consolidation of the

Anglican position. On the other side the most notable Puritan preachers of the time were Henry Smith (*d.* 1593) and William Perkins (*d.* 1602). In Scotland the redoubtable John Knox had thundered eloquently and vehemently against Rome until his death in 1572.

The sermon figured prominently in the life of the seventeenth century, among Anglicans and Puritans alike, and was usually a lengthy proceeding. Until the Restoration the Anglican preachers wrote out their sermons as a rule, and read them. The Puritans frequently wrote their sermons, too ; but they kept them free from the academic flavour and the literary conceits which offended them in Anglican sermons, and they preferred to learn their sermons by heart and to preach them from memory. The greatest names on the Anglican side were those of the spiritually minded Lancelot Andrewes (*d.* 1626), Bishop of Chichester, Ely, and Winchester, in turn ; John Donne (*d.* 1631), the famous Dean of St. Paul's ; Joseph Hall (*d.* 1656), Bishop of Exeter and of Norwich ; and Jeremy Taylor (*d.* 1667), whose sermons belong equally to religion and to literature. On the Puritan and Presbyterian side were such giants as Thomas Goodwin (*d.* 1679), John Owen (*d.* 1683), and Richard Baxter (*d.* 1691), and in Scotland Alexander Henderson (*d.* 1646), Samuel Rutherford (*d.* 1661), and David Dickson (*d.* 1663).

Of the many catechisms and forms of instruction provided during the course of the Reformation in Great Britain the most important were the Anglican *Catechism*, which was included in the Prayer-Book of 1549, supplemented in 1604 by an additional section on the sacraments, and the Calvinistic *Shorter Catechism of the Westminster Assembly*, which was adopted in 1648.

VI.—THE HALLOWING OF LIFE

1. *Festivals and Fasts.*   After making several experimental drafts of a reformed calendar Cranmer finally provided, in the 1549 Prayer-Book, for the observance of Easter Day (with the two following days), Whitsunday (with the two following days), Trinity Sunday, and all other Sundays in the year, and twenty-five Holydays.   These all rested upon the authority of the Bible, and included the feasts of our Lord, the Purification and the Annunciation of the Blessed Virgin, the Innocents, St. John Baptist, St. Mary Magdalene, St. Stephen, All Saints, and Michaelmas.   Fast-days were not provided for in the Prayer-Book, but their observance was ordered by Statutes passed in 1549 and 1552.

The 1552 Prayer-Book deleted St. Mary Magdalene ; the name of St. Barnabas was inadvertently omitted from the Kalendar, though the Collect, Epistle, and Gospel for the day were retained ; and four days were marked with the names of St. George, Lammas, St. Laurence, and St. Clement, respectively, for secular convenience and with no provision for their liturgical observance. This marks the introduction of the system of what came to be known as Black Letter days in distinction from Red Letter days.

In 1559 the Kalendar of 1552 was reproduced, with the restoration of the name of St. Barnabas and the omission of St. Clement. But in 1561 this was superseded by a new Kalendar, which extended the list of Black Letter days to a total of sixty-four, including St. Mary Magdalene among them. No liturgical observance of these days was prescribed ; and it appears that they were included for the convenience of those who had learned to know them as familiar landmarks, and so that they might not be altogether condemned to oblivion.

St. Enurchus was added to the list in 1604, and St. Alban and the Venerable Bede in 1662. In the latter year descriptions were added to the names of saints ; provision was made for the special observance of the Papists' Conspiracy, the Martyrdom of King Charles the First, and the birth and return of King Charles the Second ; and instructions were given for the first time about the observance of Movable and Immovable Feasts, and Days of Fasting and Abstinence.

2. *Marriage and Childbirth.* The marriage service which was included in the First Prayer-Book was practically the same as the Sarum service, with a slight admixture of Lutheran elements ; and it was reproduced in the 1662 Book with very few changes. Whereas it had been the custom for the introductory part of the service to take place in the church porch, the bridal party was now instructed at the beginning to come " into the body of the church." The opening exhortation was enlarged by the addition of a statement of the causes for which matrimony was ordained. Following a practice which had been introduced in the late medieval period, probably in the fourteenth century, the woman's vows included a promise to obey her husband ; and the ring, which had hitherto been placed on the right hand, was now to be placed on the left hand in accordance with a growing Continental custom ; and no provision was made for blessing it. From Hermann's *Consultation* there was introduced the joining of the right hands of the man and woman after marriage, followed by a declaration of the indissolubility of marriage and a solemn pronouncement that the couple were now " man and wife together." Psalm lxvii. was pre-scribed as an alternative to Psalm cxxviii., for use during the procession to the altar, where the cus-tomary prayers were said, with some adaptation. From 1549 to 1662 it was required that the Holy

Communion should follow, and a homily was provided for use after the Gospel. In 1662 Communion was no longer prescribed, but was said to be " convenient," as a conclusion to the wedding ; and the homily was to be read at the end of the service, unless a sermon was preached.

The short service to be used after childbirth was entitled *The Order of the Purification of Women* in the 1549 Book ; but in 1552 the old idea of ceremonial defilement was abandoned and the title was changed to *The Thanksgiving of Women after Childbirth, commonly called the Churching of Women.* In 1549 it was directed that it should take place, not outside the church door, as had been the custom, but " nigh unto the quire door " ; in 1552 the instruction read " nigh unto the place where the table standeth " ; and in 1662 it became " in some convenient place, as hath been accustomed, or as the Ordinary shall direct." In order to preserve a desirable practice which had been generally kept in former days, though it lacked prescription, the 1662 Book ordered that " the woman shall come into the church decently apparelled," which meant veiled. The 1549 Book provided for the return of the chrisom when the mother came to church ; but from 1552 no further mention was made of its use at Baptism, and the provision consequently lapsed.

The service began with a short address, which, in the 1549 Book, included a reference to the Baptism of the child. A psalm followed, to be recited by the priest ; Psalm cxxi. was prescribed from 1549 until 1662, when Psalm cxvi. or Psalm cxxvii. was ordered to be used. Then came the Lesser Litany, the Lord's Prayer, Versicles and Responses, and a prayer which was altered in 1662 so as to include a thanksgiving for the life of the mother. She was expected to receive Communion afterwards.

3. *Sickness and Death.* The office of the Visitation of the Sick kept close to the use of the Middle Ages. Opening with Psalm cxliii. (omitted after 1549) and its antiphon, the Lesser Litany, the Lord's Prayer, and versicles, the priest recited two prayers translated from two of the customary nine Collects at this point, and then read an exhortation. After the Creed the sick man made his confession, or, according to the 1662 Book, was to be moved to make his confession. Prayers and Psalm lxxi. followed the absolution. In 1549 provision was then made for unction, but this was omitted in 1552. In 1662 four prayers were added for particular cases.

In 1549 it was permitted to the priest to carry from the church to the sick man's house a reserved portion of the Elements which had been consecrated that day, if a celebration of the Holy Communion had taken place. If not, he must consecrate in the sick-room ; and from 1552 onwards provision was made for this method alone. A special Collect, Epistle, and Gospel were provided ; the Creed and the Exhortation were omitted ; and in 1552 the Prayer for the Church was omitted also.

The medieval order of burial was compressed and greatly changed in 1549, though the four customary parts were retained. There was the procession from the lychgate, during which three anthems were said or sung ; then there was the Office to be said in church, before or after the burial, consisting of Psalms cxvi., cxlvi., and cxxxix., a lesson from 1 Cor. xv., the Lesser Litany, the Lord's Prayer, versicles, and a concluding prayer ; with this went a celebration of the Holy Communion, for which an Introit (Psalm xlii.) and a special Collect, Epistle, and Gospel were provided ; and there was the burial, which took place during the recitation of two anthems, the commendation, a further anthem, and two prayers. In 1552 there were various omissions and a confused reconstruction of the parts of the service, suggesting an uncertain state of mind. The service began with the three anthems used in procession ; the two anthems at the grave followed ; then came the commendation, changed into a committal, followed by an anthem but not by prayers ; the psalms were omitted ; the lesson was followed by the Lesser Litany, the Lord's Prayer, a prayer which included an indirect intercession for the dead person, and the Collect intended for use at the Holy Communion but without any reference to a celebration of the Eucharist. In 1662 there was a clearer division of the service between the church and the graveside, Psalms xxxix. and xc. were inserted, and all suggestion of prayer for the dead disappeared.

VII.——POPULAR DEVOTIONS

The popular devotions which had multiplied greatly during the Middle Ages, concentrating especially upon the Blessed Virgin and the Blessed Sacrament, were abolished during the Reformation by three means. Relics, images, and shrines, on which they had largely depended, were destroyed and forbidden ; Bible teaching was provided in the place of encouragement to superstitious practice ; and the attempt was made to direct the spiritual energies of the people away from supplementary devotions into the main stream of the Church's worship. There was inevitably a sense of loss and of grievance in many quarters, and some active protests were made ; but the leaven of the new learning worked with speed, and increasing prosperity reconciled many to the changed attitude towards the saints and to the conversion of Holydays into working-days.

CHAPTER VII

THE COUNTER-REFORMATION AND AFTER

I.—A SURVEY OF THE PERIOD

The Protestant Reformation in Germany and Switzerland and in the other Continental States to which it spread was countered by Rome by means of theological argument, papal and conciliar action, the revival of the Inquisition, resort to burnings and wholesale massacres, and by military warfare. It should be noted, however, not only that Rome had no monopoly in some of these things, but that it was countered also by a movement of reform in morals and piety. In Italy, after the death of Leo X in 1521, there was a strong reaction against the laxity produced by the Renaissance. Reforms were instituted by great spiritual leaders such as St. Charles Borromeo, Cardinal Archbishop of Milan, and St. Philip Neri, founder of the Oratorians; new religious orders were established; and there arose a succession of high-minded and zealous Popes who strove to recover the Church's losses. In Spain, which made bitter use of the Inquisition, there was also the pure devotion, the Catholic loyalty, and the missionary zeal, of St. Ignatius Loyola, who won the Pope's approval of his Society of Jesus in 1540;

of St. Francis Xavier, who burnt himself out in ministering to the peoples of the Far East; and of St. Teresa of Avila, who reformed the Carmelites, founded thirty religious houses, and wrote precious treatises on the life of prayer.   In France, with its black record of persecution and massacre, which reached its climax in the slaughter of eight thousand Huguenots on St. Bartholomew's Day in 1572, there came a little later the noble life of St. Francis de Sales (1567–1622) with its golden promise of French Catholic culture and piety in the seventeenth century, and the extraordinary work of charity and evangelism carried out by St. Vincent de Paul (1576–1660).

There was, however, little or nothing of doctrinal reform, the Council of Trent, which sat, with intervals, from 1545 to 1563, reasserting the beliefs of the medieval Church and anathematizing those who rejected them.   There was a greater insistence upon uniformity of worship, a central authority of direction and reference being provided by the institution of the Congregation of Rites in 1588.   There was a strict reform of discipline; and there was an increase in the number of those who desired to exalt the papacy as the sole organ of government in the Church and the stronghold of Catholicism against the sectional hostilities of Protestantism. Great developments were to follow, in doctrine, in forms of devotion, and even in papal claims ; but the medieval Church of the West, shorn of the various Protestant bodies which had separated themselves from it, and of the reformed Church of England, had already become in effect the *Roman* Catholic Church of modern times.

In the seventeenth century Roman Catholicism gained ground. The Peace of Westphalia, which ended the Thirty Years' War in 1648, granted liberty of conscience to the Protestants ; but by the end of the century large numbers of the German people had abandoned Lutheranism and given their allegiance to Rome. Poland exchanged its Calvinism and Socinianism for Catholicism, and formed a Uniat Church. Spain remained solidly steadfast ; and there was a good prospect of a large part of America being added to the Roman Church through Spanish zeal. In France the liberty which had been allowed to the Huguenots in 1598 by the Edict of Nantes was withdrawn in 1685, and they were harried and expelled from the country. It was France, however, that presented two serious oppositions to Rome in its Jansenism and Gallicanism, the former of which taught a doctrine of grace which was resisted with all the strength of the Jesuits, while the latter opposed itself to the Ultramontanism of those who desired the complete exaltation of the papacy. In England Roman Catholicism maintained its existence under strict limitations and without power.

The eighteenth century brought many troubles to Rome and witnessed a marked decline in its effectiveness. An increasing spirit of worldliness recorded itself in its architecture and music and in much of its preaching ; and St. Alphonsus Liguori, who lived from 1696 to 1787 and was canonized in 1839, introduced dogmatic novelties and new forms of devotion which have since become characteristic of Roman Catholicism, and render it extremely vulnerable to Catholic criticism. The Jansenist Church of Utrecht broke away from Rome in 1723. The Jesuits came into great disfavour and were expelled from Portugal in 1759, from France in 1764, and from Spain in 1767, the Pope suppressing them formally but quite ineffectually in 1773. Febronianism in Germany and Josephism in Austria arose in the second half of the century as expressions of the same national spirit as was seen in the continuing Gallicanism of the French Church. And in England, where there was a further decrease in the small number of those who gave their loyalty to Rome, the Vicars Apostolic, or episcopal stewards of the Pope, who tended the little flock, presented a memorable Protestation to the Government in 1789, in which they gave expression to the spirit of Gallicanism and explicitly denied the suggestion of belief in papal infallibility.

The nineteenth century was marked by a revival in the fortunes of the Roman Church and by the progress and triumph of Ultramontanism, even in France, where the opening years of the century saw the reconstitution of the Church out of the chaos produced by the Revolution. In England the Catholic Emancipation Act of 1829 brought relief to the Roman Catholics, who began to increase in numbers, and in 1850 were placed under the care of an archbishop and twelve suffragan bishops with territorial jurisdiction. Two outstanding events in the century were the papal definition of the Immaculate Conception of the Blessed Virgin in 1854 and the conciliar promulgation of the dogma of Papal Infallibility in 1870. In the latter case the decision of the Vatican Council was attended with a considerable measure of dissent inside the Roman Church, though with the small resulting loss of the " Old Catholics " in Germany and Switzerland.

II.—ESTATES OF MEN AND THEIR FUNCTIONS IN WORSHIP

1. *The Laity.* The Roman Church continued unchanged the relative parts played by clergy and layfolk in the worship of the Middle Ages. Not forgetting that the laity share in the Church's priestly character and ministry, and retaining in its liturgical formulæ phrases which clearly imply the co-opera-

tion of the Faithful even in the sacrifice of the Mass,
in practice it continued to lay all the stress upon the
priesthood of the ministerial priest and to require of
the laity a devout attendance at worship rather than
an active co-operation, except in the case of lay persons chosen to discharge subordinate ministerial
functions.   Until recent times the independent performance of supplementary devotions was encouraged, rather than a sustained attention to the matter
in hand ; and the variety of the devotions used was
steadily increased.   But a Liturgical Movement, in
which the Benedictines are playing a great part, is at
present seeking to concentrate attention on the
Mass itself.

2. *The Clergy and their Assistants.*   The major
and minor orders were all retained by Rome, the
subdiaconate being accounted a major order though
not included within the sacrament of Holy Orders ;
and the requirement of celibacy was continued.
The Council of Florence having erroneously declared in 1439 that the *traditio instrumentorum*
constituted the "matter" of ordination, the
ceremonies belonging to it were retained, and
until recently they were thus regarded.   The
customary vestments and dress of the clergy all
continued in use, though commonly in debased
and excessively ornamented forms until the reform movement of recent years.   The character-

istic peaked *biretta* was introduced in the sixteenth
century.

3. *The Religious Orders.* The multiplication of
Orders, Clerks Regular, Societies, Congregations,
and Brotherhoods, has been a marked feature of the
post-Reformation history of the Roman Church,
and has been at once a testimony to the devotion of
its members, an increase to its worshipping life and
to its educational and missionary power, and something of an embarrassment at times to its central
authority in the matter of co-ordination and
disciplinary control.

III.—PLACES OF WORSHIP; AND LITURGICAL BOOKS AND MUSIC

1. *Places of Worship.* The custom arose in the
sixteenth century of having a *tabernaculum*, or small
chest, fixed on the middle of the altar to hold the
reserved Elements, instead of the cupboard in the
north wall or the hanging pyx which had been
previously used.

From the end of the sixteenth century to the third
quarter of the eighteenth century Roman Catholic
churches were usually built in that degenerate and
pretentious style which is known as Baroque, and
their interiors were floridly decorated with rococo
ornamentation. They were arranged so as to serve
primarily as a setting for the Mass, and had, there-

fore, a broad nave permitting a clear view of the high altar with its elaborately contrived surroundings, while chapels with their lesser altars were placed in the aisles. From the last quarter of the eighteenth century there was a return to older and more worthy forms of architecture, and the Gothic style once more came into favour.

2. *Liturgical Books and Music.* The Roman Rite was thoroughly revised in the sixteenth century, and was issued piecemeal in six official books, *Breviarium Romanum* in 1568, *Missale Romanum* in 1570, *Martyrologium Romanum* in 1583, *Pontificale Romanum* in 1596, *Caeremoniale Episcoporum* in 1600, and *Rituale Romanum* in 1614. Authoritative changes have been made in these books at various times since then, and it is recognized that they remain subject to further modification. The considerable changes made in France without the authority of the Pope during " the liturgical deviation " which began in the latter part of the seventeenth century were gradually eliminated between the years 1830 and 1853. The *Memoriale rituum*, published in 1725 for the smaller parish churches of Rome, and prescribed for general use in 1821, is in the nature of a supplement to the Missals and provides a simplified form of Mass. Books known as *paroissiens*, containing translations and explanations of extracts from the missal and the breviary for the use of the laity, are

being increasingly used as a result of the Liturgical Movement.

It is permitted to some of the Religious Orders to vary the Roman Rite in some particulars according to their historic usage ; the Ambrosian Rite is allowed to the archdiocese of Milan, and the Mozarabic Rite to Toledo ; and there is a total of sixteen different Rites permitted to the Uniat Churches in the East, in eleven different languages. Thus there are altogether nineteen Rites authorized by Rome and twelve liturgical languages.

A rigorous reform of Church music was undertaken in the sixteenth century with the object of restoring the purity of plain-chant and of securing that, where polyphony was used, musical renderings should never be allowed to obscure the text. The first object was not truly achieved until the second half of the nineteenth century, when the abbey of Solesmes was made famous by the labours of Dom Pothier and Dom Mocquereau. The second object was gained for a time, but was completely lost in the eighteenth century, when the concert-hall invaded the church, and great composers, such as Haydn and Mozart, Bach and Beethoven, interpreted the rite with noble music which lacked liturgical value. Strong reaction set in again, however, in the middle of the nineteenth century, and a drastic reform has once more been instituted.

IV.—INITIATION AND ECCLESIASTICAL DISCIPLINE

1. *Initiation.*   After some uncertainty about the length of the interval between Baptism and Confirmation in the case of children, Rome decided in favour of a normal gap of seven years.   The parish priest remained responsible for Baptism and the bishop for Confirmation, with the subsequent provision in the latter case that missionary priests might be specially empowered to confirm, and that the same privilege might be permitted to priests ministering in the Uniat Churches of the East, in conformity with the general Eastern practice.   A godfather or godmother other than the parents was required both at Baptism and at Confirmation, both being allowed at the former, but only one at the latter.

At Baptism the child is held by the godmother throughout the service, which takes place in three stages.   In the first part, at the church door, the interrogations and ceremonies of the ancient catechumenate are summarily performed ; in the second part there is a procession towards, but not up to, the font, during which the Creed and the Lord's Prayer are recited, and, when the procession has halted, the priest performs the exorcism, the Effeta, and an anointing ; and the third part, at the font, is the actual baptism and chrismation.   The administration of Confirmation is begun by a brief invocation of the Holy Spirit, and the extension of the bishop's hands over the candidates, while he prays for the sevenfold gift. Then the bishop confirms the candidates in turn, laying his hand on the head of each and simultaneously anointing the forehead with his thumb, previously dipped in chrism, after which he gives him a light blow on the left cheek, saying *Pax tecum*. Prayers follow, and a special blessing.

2. *Ecclesiastical Discipline*. The medieval disciplinary system was continued by Rome, the practice of granting indulgences being defended by the Council of Trent, though it recognized the existence of abuses and recommended moderation in its use. The introduction of confessionals by St. Charles Borromeo immediately after the conclusion of the Council led to the general abandonment of the former use of a chair in the choir or behind the altar. In the seventeenth century confession was greatly encouraged by the Jesuits, whose casuistry provoked hostile criticism within and without the Roman Church, most notably that of Pascal ; but the resultant Equiprobabilism of St. Alphonsus Liguori in the eighteenth century was looked upon with approval by Rome in the following century, so that a man who desires to follow the less strict of two courses of action is held to be justified in doing so if he can achieve something approaching a balance of

authorities for and against it. This is, however, but a small part of the whole system of spiritual and moral direction and of the administration of the sacrament of penance; and on a general view of that system it must be recognized that Rome stands supreme in post-Reformation Christendom in her careful maintenance of discipline and in the thoroughness and competence with which she seeks to assist the moral and spiritual progress of her members.

V.—CORPORATE WORSHIP

1. *The Mass.* The Roman Church has consistently regarded the Mass as the heart of its worshipping life, holding its celebration to be the primary function of the priesthood and attendance at its celebration to be the chief duty of the laity. It has consistently maintained the medieval doctrine of Transubstantiation; and, though divergences have appeared in the interpretations of the sacrifice of the Mass put forth by its theologians, the popular conception of the medieval period remains the popular conception of to-day.

The medieval rite has been changed hardly at all. To the eleven Proper Prefaces which were retained in 1570 four have since been added—one for Requiem Masses in 1919, one for the Mass of St. Joseph in the same year, one for the feast of Christ

the King in 1927, and one for the feast of the Sacred
Heart in 1929. In 1570 the customary reading of
" the Last Gospel " (John i. 1–14) by the celebrant
after Mass was reckoned as a part of the Mass itself.
In 1884 prayers were prescribed to be recited by the
celebrant with the people after Low Masses ; and
the threefold invocation of the Sacred Heart was
subsequently added to them.

At Low Mass the priest must always be attended
by a server. When Mass is sung and the celebrant
is unattended by deacon and subdeacon it is known
as *Missa Cantata* ; but if he is supported by the
other sacred ministers it is called *Solemn* or *High
Mass*. In the latter case incense is used and the
ceremonial is more elaborate. On certain days it is
permitted to say Mass with a formulary which is not
of the day, with special intention or as an act of
special devotion. This is known as a *Votive Mass*.
Two Masses may be permitted to a priest by
episcopal authority on Sundays and Holydays, if this
is judged to be necessary to meet the needs of the
Faithful ; and three Masses are said on Christmas
Day and All Souls' Day. But the general rule is
that every priest should say Mass once daily.

The frequent reception of the Blessed Sacrament
has been much encouraged of recent years, the
almost invariable rule that the communicant should
fast from food and drink from midnight being

strictly observed.   Communion is administered in
one kind only, except in some of the Uniat Churches;
and the Bread is placed by the priest upon the communicant's tongue, the use of the hands in receiving
being forbidden.   By means of Reservation, which
is practised in all cathedral and parish churches,
Communion may be received out of Mass by both
sick and whole.

2. *The Daily Office*.   Of the early attempts that
were made to reform the medieval Breviary the
most important was that of Cardinal Quignon,
which appeared in 1535.   In his Breviary of Holy
Cross provision was made for the weekly recitation
of the whole Psalter ; scriptural lessons were
lengthened so as to admit of the greater part of the
Bible being read once in each year and the Pauline
Epistles twice ; versicles and responses were rejected and many of the hymns also.   After enjoying
considerable popularity this Breviary was suppressed in 1558 by means of an order that it should
not be reprinted.   Ten years later an official revision
of the medieval Breviary appeared, which was more
conservative than Quignon's.   It reduced the
length of the swollen Office by providing that the
Office of the Dead should be recited only once a
month and the Office of our Lady on Saturdays
only ; it made modest improvements in the arrange-
ments for the recitation of the Psalter and the read-

ing of the Bible; and it clarified the interpretation of the accumulated rubrical directions. Changes were made subsequently in this Breviary, especially by Baronius and Bellarmine under the direction of Clement VIII in 1602, and in 1632 by Urban VIII, who with questionable taste corrected many of the hymns; independent reform was undertaken in France as an outcome of the spirit of Gallicanism, so that from 1670 to the middle of the nineteenth century there were several variations in use in French dioceses; a projected reform by Benedict XIV (*d.* 1758) proved abortive; and a thorough and most necessary reform, initiated by the Pope in 1913 and beginning with the Psalter, is still in progress.

While the members of communities perform the Daily Office in its seven parts at intervals during the day and night, the secular clergy are accustomed to make two or three groups of those parts in their private recitation of them. When parts of the Office are publicly recited, no very strict regard is paid to their proper hour. This is seen, for example, in the service of *Tenebrae*, at which Mattins and Lauds are recited together on the evenings of Wednesday, Thursday, and Friday in Holy Week. Vespers is the only part of the Office which is frequented by the laity, some of whom are accustomed to attend it on Sundays and Holydays and their eves.

3. *Litanies and Processions.* In view of the character of many of the petitions which had found their way into the Church's litanies, Benedict XIV forbad the liturgical use of all but two of them, the Litany of the Saints and the Litany of the Blessed Virgin, which is also known as the Litany of the Loreto. To these have been added in recent times the Litany of the Holy Name of Jesus, the Litany of the Sacred Heart of Jesus, and the Litany of St. Joseph.

The use of penitential processions on St. Mark's Day, the Rogation Days, Good Friday, and All Souls' Day, has continued; and processions of praise and thanksgiving have preserved the medieval custom of carrying the Blessed Sacrament (a practice particularly associated with the observance of Corpus Christi) and images of the saints.

4. *Preaching and Teaching.* The Roman Catechism, which is known as the Catechism of the Council of Trent, appeared in 1566, three years after the conclusion of the Council. It contains an authoritative summary of the findings of the Council, prepared for the guidance of parish priests in their work of teaching, and arranged in four divisions dealing respectively with Faith, the Means of Grace, the Decalogue, and the Lord's Prayer. Special attention to the teaching of the young was given by the Society of Jesus from its earliest days, and its zeal

has been emulated by many Orders founded during the post-Reformation period. While the sermon was still subordinated to the liturgy, there was a vigorous repudiation of heresy and a general use of the vernacular, so that the importance of the sermon was increased in the eyes of the people. The private use of the Bible by the laity was carefully controlled by authority, and it cannot be said to have been encouraged until quite recent times.

In the sixteenth century some of the best-known preachers were the Franciscan John Wild (*d.* 1554), and the Jesuit Peter Canisius (*d.* 1597), in Germany; Cornelio Musso (*d.* 1575) in Italy; and Villanova (*d.* 1555), Juan de Avila (*d.* 1569), and Luiz de Granada (*d.* 1588) in Spain, all three possessed of unusual eloquence and great devotion.

In seventeenth-century Germany Abraham of Santa Clara (*d.* 1709) was prominent among a number of considerable preachers. Italy produced a crop of affected and bombastic preachers during the first half of the century, until reaction and reform were promoted by Paolo Segneri (*d.* 1694). Portugal delighted in the learning and the moving eloquence of Antonio Vieyra (*d.* 1697). And France, which was adorned by St. Francis de Sales (*d.* 1622) in the early part of the century, rose to supreme heights in its latter half, when Louis Bourdaloue (*d.* 1704), Jacques Bénigne Bossuet (*d.* 1704), François Fénelon (*d.* 1715), and other lesser but great preachers gave to the French pulpit unprecedented glory and fame.

Preaching power declined in the eighteenth century, even in France, though the name of Jean Baptiste Massillon (*d.* 1742) must be classed with the great names just mentioned. In the nineteenth century, however, there was a steady revival of power; and among a host of memorable preachers some outstanding names are those of Jean Baptiste Henri Lacordaire (*d.* 1861), Auguste Gratry (*d.* 1872), Felix Dupanloup (*d.* 1878), Henri Didon (*d.* 1900), and Père Hyacinthe (*d.* 1912), in France, and Nicholas Wiseman (*d.* 1865), Henry Edward Manning (*d.* 1892), and John Henry Newman (*d.* 1890), in England.

VI.—THE HALLOWING OF LIFE

1. *Festivals and Fasts.* The calendar of the Roman Church has been subjected to an almost continuous process of revision. By the action of successive Popes feasts have sometimes been suppressed, lapsed festivals have been restored, new festivals have been introduced, and an exact system of classification has been evolved.

A little before the Reformation period the Feast of the Transfiguration was instituted in 1457. In the Roman Breviary of 1568 changes were made, chiefly by omissions and by reductions of rank, so that as a result about one hundred days of the Office of the Time were occupied by the Offices of the Saints. The Feast of the Most Holy Rosary was introduced by Gregory XIII in 1571 ; a number of rejected feasts reappeared under Sixtus V (d. 1590) ; and numerous alterations, chiefly in the matter of classification, were effected by Clement VIII (d. 1605). In 1683 the Feast of the Holy Name of Mary was introduced by Innocent XI. The Feast of the Immaculate Conception of the Blessed Virgin, which had been observed by the Franciscan Order from 1263, was extended to the Church by Clement XI in 1708 ; and the Feast of the Holy Name of Jesus was similarly extended by Benedict XIII in 1721. The Feast of the Seven Dolours of the Blessed Virgin, already observed on the Friday of Passion Week, was duplicated in 1814 by Pius VII, who ordered its observance to be repeated in September. In 1847 Pius IX instituted the Feast of the Patronage of St. Joseph ; and in 1856 he extended to the Church the observance of the Feast of the Sacred Heart of Jesus, which had been granted to particular churches by Clement XIII in 1765. The Feast of Our Lady of Lourdes, or the Apparition of the Blessed Mary Immaculate, was instituted to commemorate the first of the eighteen appearances of the Virgin at Lourdes in 1858. In 1925 the Feast of Christ the King was ordained by Pius XI.

All feasts are divided into two classes, feasts of precept and feasts of devotion. The former are holydays on which the Faithful in most Catholic countries refrain from unnecessary servile labour and attend Mass. These include all the Sundays in the year, Christmas Day, the Circumcision, the Epiphany, the Ascension, Corpus Christi, the Immaculate Conception and the Assumption of the Blessed Virgin, St. Joseph, St. Peter and St. Paul, and All Saints. The feasts of devotion, which form the second division, are purely ecclesiastical feasts, and are of three grades, double, semi-double, and simple. " Double " feasts, which were so called because of the recitation of the double Office, of the feast and of the ferial (or regular Office of the day), are graded in four classes as doubles of the first class, doubles of the second class, major doubles, and minor doubles.

2. *Marriage and Childbirth.* The full marriage rite includes the nuptial Mass ; but at certain ecclesiastical seasons, and in the case of mixed marriages and in some other cases, the rite is shorn of the Mass and, consequently, of the nuptial blessing which belongs to it. Apart from various permitted local customs, the essential rite is very simple and brief. It includes a declaration of consent on the part of the bridegroom and then of the bride, in response to questions put by the priest ; the joining of their

right hands, a declaration by the priest that he unites them in matrimony in the Name of the Trinity, and the sprinkling of the couple with holy water; the blessing of the ring, which is asperged and then placed by the man upon the woman's ring-finger in the Name; and the recitation of versicles and a prayer by the priest.

A woman who comes to give thanks and to seek a blessing after childbirth kneels at the church door and holds a lighted candle. Having sprinkled her with holy water, the priest recites the psalm *Domini est terra*, and afterwards leads her into church holding in her hand the left end of the white stole which he wears for the occasion. When they reach the appointed altar, the priest recites the *Kyrie*, the Lord's Prayer, a number of versicles, and a prayer for blessing; and he then sprinkles the woman again with holy water and pronounces a blessing.

3. *Sickness and Death*. Ministrations to the sick, which are practically the same as in the Middle Ages, include prayers for the restoration of health, sprinkling with holy water, the hearing of the sick man's confession, the administration of the Holy Communion, and particular blessings. The priest carries the *viaticum* from church either in public procession or privately, reciting psalms on his way to the house; and, having arrived, he sprinkles the sick man with holy water, recites the Asperges,

administers the Sacrament, and concludes with prayers.

When death is thought to be near, confession and Communion are followed by Extreme Unction, though not as a rule on the same day. After a short address of consolation and instruction and the recitation of prayers, the priest anoints the eyes, ears, nostrils, mouth, hands, and feet of the sick person, while those who are present join in the recitation of penitential psalms and a litany or prayers. A special litany and prayers are used by the priest at the time of the soul's departure.

The full order of burial includes the processional conveyance of the body to church, preceded by the priest, while psalms are recited ; the saying of the Office of the Dead, which consists of Mattins and Lauds ; the Requiem Mass, after which a funeral oration may be preached ; the Absolution, with the sprinkling of the coffin ; and the actual interment. Some or all of the first four parts may be omitted, when necessary ; but great importance is attached to the Requiem Mass, the medieval conceptions of Purgatory and of the efficacy of Masses for the Dead persisting unchanged.

VI.—POPULAR DEVOTIONS

The medieval churchman owed many of his devotional exercises to the inventiveness of the Franciscans; the Roman Catholic is further indebted to the Jesuits, and to the eighteenth-century Italian bishop, St. Alphonsus Liguori, who founded the Order of Redemptorists and exercised a remarkable influence on the disciplinary system of the Roman Church and on the devotional life of its members. The popular devotions of Roman Catholics are directed to our Lord, to the Blessed Sacrament, and to the Blessed Virgin Mary and all the saints.

The devotion in honour of the Sacred Heart of Jesus, which is observed on the first Friday in each month, is connected by some with the medieval devotion to the Five Wounds of our Lord; but it substitutes for a mystical response to the sacrificial love of Christ the worship of His physical Heart, and it dates only from the latter half of the seventeenth century. The medieval devotion of the Way of the Cross, known as the Stations of the Cross, is very popular, and bestows indulgences upon those who meditate at each of the fourteen stations. The use of the crucifix and of the sacred sign at times of prayer is general.

The Blessed Sacrament, which is reserved in all parish churches for the Communion of sick and whole, is the focus of much private devotion, and also of corporate devotions at Benediction. At this very popular service the " Sanctissimum " is taken from the tabernacle on the altar and exposed in a monstrance, with which the priest makes the sign of the cross over the people.   Prolonged exposition of the Host is allowed at certain times in order to provide opportunity for devotion and prayer and stimulation to the same, the chief occasion of this being the Forty Hours' Prayer in remembrance of the approximate time during which our Lord's Body rested in the tomb.   Beginning and ending with a procession of the Blessed Sacrament, this includes continuous exposition for a period of roughly forty hours, usually from High Mass on the first day to the conclusion of High Mass on the third day.

Candles are lighted before images of the saints and their aid is invoked, doubtless with widely differing conceptions of their power and manner of lending assistance, according to the understanding of the worshipper ; special forms of devotion are associated with particular saints, such as the observance of Thirteen Tuesdays in honour of St. Antony of Padua and Six Sundays in honour of St. Aloysius ; devotions to the Blessed Virgin Mary claim a large part of the attention and time of every devout Roman Catholic, especially in the months of May and October ; and pilgrimages to shrines and holy places are believed to be of great efficacy for the healing of soul and body alike.

CHAPTER VIII

NON-ROMAN CHRISTENDOM SINCE
THE REFORMATION

The schism of 1054 divided the Church into two parts—the Holy Orthodox Church of the East (with its separated nationalist groups), and the Catholic Church of the West. The Reformation left that division untouched, and further divided the western half into three parts, characterized respectively by a Roman Catholicism, a non-Roman Catholicism, and an anti-Catholic Protestantism. Thus, while the Roman Catholic section of Christendom claims that it alone is the true Church and that all other Christians are schismatics or heretics, the claim is countered on three sides; and the worship of God through Jesus Christ is carried on outside the Roman Church by the Orthodox, who show a marked adherence to the Church's oldest liturgical forms and a power of other-worldly beauty and measured solemnity, by the Anglicans and some of the Lutherans, who in their different ways have purged medieval worship of its corruptions and have adapted it to the modern age, and by a number of Protestant bodies, who claim to have reverted to a primitive simplicity of form earlier than Catholicism. If to the second group we add the Old Catholics, the most recent adherents to non-Roman Catholicism, we shall be in a position to cover the whole field of non-Roman worship in a rapid survey.

I.—THE HOLY ORTHODOX CHURCH

Abortive efforts to reunite Orthodox and Catholics were made in 1254 at the Council of Lyons, and again in 1439 at the Council of Florence. In the sixteenth century some correspondence took place between Reformers and Eastern authorities without result. Since that time Western interest in the East has been aroused periodically ; and during the past hundred years much has been done to pave the way for reunion between Anglicans and Orthodox. Meanwhile the great Orthodox Church has persisted in the old ways with very little change, particularly in its worship, and it remains an important and powerful section of Christendom. In spite of prolonged persecution in Soviet Russia, a large part of the vast population of that country remains loyal to the Orthodox Church to-day ; and, though the actual numbers are uncertain, the Russian Church is still the largest of the autocephalous members of the Orthodox Communion. Next in size is the Roumanian Church, with some 13 million people. Then come Greece and Yugo-Slavia, with 6 million

each, and Bulgaria with 5 million.   Large Orthodox
minorities are found among the peoples of Poland,
Finland, Esthonia, Lithuania, and Latvia.   And the
great dispersion settled in America and elsewhere
brings the total membership of the Orthodox
Church up to more than 100 million people.

The threefold ministry of the Church is retained
by the Orthodox, with an effective diaconate.
Parochial priests and deacons are required to be
married men ; bishops, on the contrary, are drawn
from the monastic order and are celibate.   The only
Minor Orders used are those of reader or chanter,
and subdeacon.   While church buildings vary
greatly in architectural style in the different Orthodox lands, their internal arrangement usually pre-
serves the ancient threefold division into narthex,
nave, and sanctuary, though the disappearance of
the catechumenate has led to the loss of the first of
these in some places.   The nave, which is not
equipped with seats, is separated from the sanctuary
by a solid screen of stone or wood, adorned with
icons, or sacred pictures, and known in consequence
as the iconostasis.   This is pierced by three doors ;
the Royal Doors in the middle, hung with a curtain
on the inside, opening on the cubical altar which
stands within ; the Servers' door on the left, opening on the table of prothesis and used for the processions of the Little Entrance and the Great

Entrance; and the Deacon's door on the right, providing for the passage of that minister to and from the sanctuary during the celebration of the liturgy. Immediately west of the screen there is sometimes a platform for the use of the deacon and the members of the choir, whose singing is always unaccompanied. All services are in the vernacular.

The twofold rite of initiation is administered to infants at the font by the parish priest, who anoints with oil blessed by the bishop, in place of episcopal Confirmation by the laying on of hands. Priestly absolution is sought by penitents, yearly at the least, and is pronounced in the precatory form.

The Eucharist is celebrated on Sundays and holy-days, with its full liturgical and ceremonial setting, once only at the single altar which each church possesses. There is no equivalent to the Low Mass of the West, nor is the Eucharist celebrated daily. The liturgy generally used is that of St. John Chrysostom; but the Liturgy of St. Basil is used on the Feast of St. Basil, Christmas Eve, the Eve of the Epiphany, the first five Sundays in Lent, Maundy Thursday and Easter Eve: and the Liturgy of the Presanctified is used on the Wednesdays and Fridays in Lent, and on Monday, Tuesday, and Wednesday in Holy Week. Sermons are infrequent. Leavened bread is used; and the Communion is administered in both kinds, by intinction. The Sacrament is invariably reserved in both kinds on the altar ; but the use of Benediction and Exposition is unknown.

The Orthodox Daily Office is composed of the customary Hours, which are recited at their appointed times by the monks but are grouped by the parish priests, usually in three daily services. Mattins, Lauds, and Prime are said in the early morning ; Terce and Sext follow later in the morning, preceding the liturgy when it is used ; and None, Vespers, and Compline are said in the evening. In form the Orthodox Hours are longer and more complicated than those used in the West.

II.—NON-ROMAN CATHOLICISM

1. *The Anglican Communion.* With the help of Wren and his followers the Church of England built many new churches in the classical style during the second half of the seventeenth century ; and, though it did not altogether deliver itself from the influence of Puritanism in its worship, the Prayer-Book of 1662 was for the most part loyally used. Charles II became a secret convert to Roman Catholicism in 1669. His brother, who succeeded him as James II in 1685, openly supported Rome ; and his obvious determination to bring England once more into allegiance to the Pope led to the peaceful Revolution of 1688, when William, Prince of Orange, was invited to succeed him on the

throne, and James fled to France. As a result of the arrival of a Dutch Calvinist with Latitudinarian sympathies the Toleration Act was passed in 1689, granting liberty of worship to all except Unitarians and Roman Catholics ; an unsuccessful attempt was made to revise the Prayer-Book in the same year, when many changes in a Protestant direction were proposed ; episcopacy was once more disestablished in Scotland, though " Episcopals " were in a considerable majority ; and grievous loss was caused to the Church of England by the secession of nine bishops and about four hundred priests, known as Nonjurors, who held that their oath of allegiance to James II precluded them from yielding obedience to William III. This Nonjuring body continued its separate existence as a part of the Catholic Church, and maintained its Catholic ideals of worship without interruption for more than a hundred years, its dwindling numbers reaching exhaustion point early in the nineteenth century. Its most important contribution to Anglican liturgical literature was the English Nonjuring Office of Holy Communion, which appeared in 1718. This borrowed largely from Scottish and Eastern sources; and it made provision for the " Usages," as they were called, of the Mixed Chalice, the Commemoration of the Departed, the Invocation, and the Oblation.

The eighteenth century, which was covered by the reigns of Queen Anne and the first three Georges, was by no means the dead period for the Church which many have supposed it to be. Not only did the Nonjurors present the best side of the Catholicism of the Church from which they went out, but within that Church itself the standards of the Book of Common Prayer were faithfully maintained by some of its members. Yet it is true that after the reign of Queen Anne (1702–1714), when less than five per cent. of the people absented themselves from the Church's worship, there was a serious increase of worldliness and laxity among clergy and laity alike, and in many a parish the worship of the Church fell far short of the requirements of the Prayer-Book. Deism and Arianism were weakening faith ; manners were coarse ; the multitudes were untended. The parish churches were filled with immense pews, and a two- or three-decker pulpit dwarfed the Communion-table, which was not served with the frequency contemplated by the Book of Common Prayer. While it was a common practice among the well-to-do to communicate on the first Sunday of every month, and numbers were often large on those days, Communion was much neglected by the rest. Morning Prayer had succeeded in substituting itself for the Eucharist as the chief act of Sunday worship. Tate and Brady's " New Version " of the psalms, issued in 1696, was in general use ; choirs led the singing from west galleries ; and accompaniment was provided by a small orchestra of amateur musicians, till this was displaced by a barrel-organ or by a harmonium.

The evangelistic work of the two Wesleys and George Whitefield at Oxford in 1729 heralded the remarkable spiritual campaign which they carried on from 1738, beginning from within the Church, but reaching positions which necessitated the departure of their Methodist or Wesleyan followers and greatly augmented the forces of Dissent ; while other Evangelicals contemporary with John Wesley, such as Fletcher, Walker, and Venn, proved to be the leaders of a movement which was not lost to the Church but provided it with a stimulus not only to pious living, but also to missionary endeavour overseas. The Church Missionary Society and the Religious Tract Society were founded in 1799, and the British and Foreign Bible Society followed in 1804. These greatly extended the work of the Society for Promoting Christian Knowledge and the Society for the Propagation of the Gospel, which had been founded as far back as 1698 and 1701 respectively. To Robert Raikes belongs the credit of strengthening, in 1780, the small beginnings which had been made in the establishment of Sunday Schools for the children of the poor.

In America, whither colonists had carried both Anglicanism and Nonconformity in the seventeenth century, there was a " Great Awakening " parallel to the Methodist movement in England and largely assisted by George Whitefield. Its results were dissipated, however, by the War of Independence (1775-1783); and towards the end of the century the Unitarians had made a marked advance. The Episcopalians, whose appeals for a bishop were long refused by the Government, received in 1785 Bishop Seabury, who had been consecrated by three Scottish bishops at Aberdeen in the previous year. Bishops White and Provoost followed in 1787, having been consecrated at Lambeth; and the first American consecration took place in 1792. Liturgical worship was continued by the American Church on Anglican lines, the 1662 Book of Common Prayer being revised in 1789 with borrowings from the Scottish Liturgy of 1637 and 1764; and it was supplemented by the addition of the Ordinal in 1792, a Form of Consecration of a Church in 1799, the Articles in 1801, and an Office of Induction or Institution in 1804. Further revisions of the book took place in 1892 and in 1928.

In Scotland the Church, which was disestablished in 1689, suffered greatly for its loyalty to the Stuarts and steadily shrank in size. Though the Prayer-Book of 1637 was not taken into use after the

Revolution, its Communion Service became popular at a later date, and the central part of the Service was printed for the people in a series of " wee bookies," the first of which appeared in 1724. The standard edition of this Liturgy appeared in 1764. The English Prayer-Book was generally used in the nineteenth century ; but in 1929 approval was given to a complete revision of the Prayer-Book, which took full account of the earlier Scottish books.

The nineteenth century witnessed a striking revival of loyalty to Prayer-Book standards in the Church of England in the face of great opposition from the authorities in Church and State. This movement began in Oxford in 1833, as Methodism had done a century earlier ; and it looked back yet another hundred years to the Anglicanism of the early part of the seventeenth century. With its insistence on the true character of the English Church and the obligation of its liturgical and disciplinary rules it combined a zeal for personal piety and, among the clergy, for the faithful discharge of the pastoral office. Newman deserted the movement and went over to the Church of Rome in 1845 ; but the work of Keble and Pusey stood firm. One of its most remarkable results was seen in the foundation of a large number of religious communities for both men and women. In the chapels of these communities and in a number of the parish churches there was a gradual recovery of eucharistic worship and of customs which had been long neglected and were almost forgotten. When this recovery was challenged by authorities, a long process of debate concerning the meaning of certain of the rubrics of the Book of Common Prayer was entered upon, legal opinion and the power of the State being invoked by the bishops. As the movement grew, the worship of the contemporary Roman Church began to be ignorantly regarded by some of the clergy as the norm for all Catholics, and foolish, not to say disloyal, borrowings were made, in complete disregard of the genius of the English rite and of true Catholic standards. The state of disorder which resulted from this led to the issue of Letters of Business to the Houses of Convocation in 1906, setting the Church the task of revising the 1662 Prayer-Book so as to meet the needs of the time, and in particular so as to equip the bishops with the necessary instrument for the proper discharge of their duty in the regulation of public worship. After long and careful work the revised book was presented to Parliament for legal sanction in 1927, and, after acceptance by the House of Lords, it was rejected by a small majority in the House of Commons. With some slight modifications it was presented to the Commons in the fol-

lowing year and was again rejected by them. The
bishops thereupon determined that, while the Book
lacked legal authorization and could not be enforced
in any of its provisions, it must be regarded as
defining the limits of permissible deviation from the
1662 Book during an emergency period and pending
a future settlement. To-day there are few churches
in the land that make no use of it. It seems certain,
however, that another attempt at revision must be
made by the Church of England before long, when
its spiritual independence has been recognized by
the State. Meanwhile the conduct of the worship
of the Church of England reveals some deplorable
eccentricities on the part of a few of its priests, a
considerable measure of amateurishness on the part
of a larger number of them, and a growing devotion
and understanding on the part of the great majority.

In Ireland the disestablished Church revised its
Prayer-Book in 1878 and again in 1926; and
similarly in the great Anglican Communion overseas the Church has revised its forms of worship
with a large measure of freedom. Canada approved
a new Prayer-Book in 1921; and South Africa has
created a revised form of Liturgy and of the
Occasional Offices, and is still engaged in a process
of piecemeal revision which began in 1911.

2. *The Old Catholics.* To the Catholics of
Utrecht, in Holland, who separated from Rome in

the eighteenth century, other small groups in Central Europe were added as a result of the declaration of papal infallibility by the Vatican Council in 1870. These Old Catholics, as they are called, vary slightly in their liturgical uses, but for the most part they keep close to the Roman rite, which they have translated into their own tongues ; and they are conservative in the matter of ceremonial. They are agreed that " the Holy Eucharist has always been the true central point of Catholic worship " ; but they hold also that " the eucharistic celebration in the Church is neither a continual repetition nor a renewal of the expiatory sacrifice which Jesus offered once for all upon the Cross."

3. *Parts of the Lutheran Church.* Though the various parts of the Lutheran Church have maintained communion with one another since the Reformation, they differ considerably in their conceptions of Church and ministry, in their practice of ministerial ordination and use, and in their forms of worship. Catholic usage has been retained in some measure in Sweden, where there was no breach in the apostolic succession of the ministry, and also in Norway, Finland, and Denmark, where an episcopate is still used, though the succession was not preserved. In Germany, where the ministry was more radically changed and the old ways were gradually abandoned, the Lutheran Church appears

to be entering on a process of liturgical recovery under the leadership of Friedrich Heiler.

The Swedish rite began to take shape in 1529, when Olaus Petri, the leading reformer, issued a *Handbook* containing forms for Baptism and the Occasional Offices. In 1531 he provided a Swedish Mass which was used at first for Low Masses only, while the Latin rite continued to be sung at High Mass. Gradually, however, the Swedish Mass ousted the Latin, taking on an enlarged and modified form in the process. The *Church Order* of Laurentius Petri, which appeared in 1571, gathered up the results of the Reformation in Sweden and provided regulations for the conduct of public worship ; but five years later King John III put out his famous Red Book, or *Liturgia Svecanae Ecclesiae catholicae et orthodoxae conformis*, which suggested to many the reversal of the work of the reformers. This was finally rejected in 1593 ; and the approved results of liturgical reform were embodied in a Prayer-Book issued in 1614, which was revised in a Protestant spirit in 1811, and again, more in conformity with the true spirit of the Swedish Reformation, in 1894.

III.—PROTESTANTISM

Of Protestantism on the Continent, in America, and particularly in Great Britain, it may be said that the love of free forms of worship, of hymn-singing and of the preaching of the Word, is no less strong to-day than it was in Reformation times. There is, however, a marked change of attitude towards liturgical services and towards the older forms of church architecture and equipment. The subject of worship is engaging the attention of Protestant scholars and students. Prejudice is slowly but surely disappearing among large numbers of the ordinary members of Protestant bodies. There is frequently to be heard a frank recognition of the regrettable loss which has been suffered through the abandonment of much of the Church's devotional treasury. And many eyes and ears are becoming gratefully aware of the aid which art and music can lend to the worship of God. Æsthetic considerations, psychological study, an educated appreciation of liturgical forms and of their relation to Christian doctrine, a widening sense of Christian brotherhood, and, above all, a growing desire to pray and to worship more worthily, are undoubtedly combining to effect a great transformation of Protestant worship, which cannot fail to play an important part in the work of reuniting Christendom.

A SUGGESTED LIBRARY OF TWENTY BOOKS FOR FURTHER STUDY

Underhill : *Worship*. Nisbet, 10s. 6d.

Oesterley : *The Jewish Background of the Christian Liturgy*. Oxford Press, 12s. 6d.

Duchesne : *Christian Worship*. S.P.C.K., 15s.

Bigg and Maclean : *The Doctrine of the Twelve Apostles*. S.P.C.K., 3s. 6d.

Easton : *The Apostolic Tradition of Hippolytus*. Cambridge Press, 7s. 6d.

Wordsworth : *Bishop Sarapion's Prayer Book*. S.P.C.K., 2s.

McClure and Feltoe : *The Pilgrimage of Etheria*. S.P.C.K., 6s.

Linton : *Twenty-five Consecration Prayers*. S.P.C.K., 7s. 6d.

Holloway : *A Study of the Byzantine Liturgy*. Mitre Press, 8s. 6d.

Swete : *Church Services and Service-books before the Reformation*. S.P.C.K., 5s.

Cabrol : *The Mass of the Western Rites*. Sands, 5s.

Cabrol : *The Roman Missal in Latin and English, with Notes*. Herder, 15s.

Brilioth : *Eucharistic Faith and Practice, Catholic and Evangelical*. S.P.C.K., 12s. 6d.

Maxwell : *An Outline of Christian Worship*. Oxford Press, 7s. 6d.

The First and Second Prayer Books of Edward VI. Dent, 2s.

The Prayer Book as Proposed in 1928. S.P.C.K., 1s. 6d.

Pullan : *The Book of Common Prayer*. Longmans, 5s.

Procter and Frere : *A New History of the Book of Common Prayer*. Macmillan, 10s. 6d.

Brightman : *The English Rite*. Longmans, 45s.

Liturgy and Worship, ed. by Lowther Clarke. S.P.C.K. 15s.

INDEX